Serious Runner's Handbook

Serious Runner's Handbook

Answers to Hundreds of Your Running Questions

By Tom Osler

ANDERSON WORLD, INC.

Mountain View, CA.

© 1978 by
Tom Osler

No information in this book may be reprinted in any
form without permission from the publisher.

World Publications, Mt. View, CA
Second Printing, November 1978
Third Printing, December 1981
Library of Congress 78-367
ISBN 0-89037-126-1

Dedicated to my wife, Kathy.

CONTENTS

FOREWORD

I owe Tom Osler more than I can ever repay by writing an introduction to his book and editing the book for him. In a sense, I owe two careers to him—one as a runner and one as a writer-editor on running.

The best thing about working together on this book is that I've been able finally to meet Tom after knowing him by his ideas for 12 years and borrowing plenty of those ideas. I've been able to thank him for it.

In running, as in other places where experimenting is going on, we have lots of cross-fertilizing of ideas. Often, we forget who planted the original seeds. So he seldom gets full credit for his work—and seldom gets a second chance to claim it as his own.

Tom Osler is such a seed-man. Back in 1966, I met his full-grown ideas at just the right time—as similar ones of my own were sprouting. He wrote a slim, roughly-produced booklet called *The Conditioning of Distance Runners*. It said some outrageous things for the time—like 90% of the running should be done at a comfortable, meandering pace. Remember, this was still the interval-training, pain-equals-gain era of running.

I was ready to accept what Tom was saying, because I'd had more than enough intervals and pain. I borrowed from

him, and from Arthur Lydiard and Ernst van Aaken,
adding my own modifications and claiming the mixture as
something original.

My booklet on the subject came out a full three years
after Tom's and added little to his except a cute name. It
sold far more copies only because it was better produced
and promoted. Other articles, booklets and books followed. But they all traced their roots back to Tom Osler.

The running world took a while to catch up with Tom.
But when it did, his ideas on combining gently-paced base
work with a period of carefully-planned sharpening for
races weren't at all outrageous anymore. They worked,
and most runners now train much like Osler—without
knowing him as one source of what they do.

Tom's little booklet grew to be a classic on training. But
those who read it found that 32 pages didn't tell them
enough. And Osler himself knew this wasn't enough space
to tell of the story that had kept evolving.

Fortunately for him and for us, he was talked into writing
at length on what he has learned since 1966. And the
book that results does several things. It gives Tom credit for
his early work and gives him a second chance to tell of it,
of course. But more important, it's a new chance to say
things that may sound outrageous now and will be accepted ways of running a few years from now.

He says stretching exercises may be dangerous. He says
walking should be a regular part of running training. The
ideal drink for long runs is heavily-sugared tea. The ultra-
marathons can be handled well by people without
superhuman ability.

Tom says these things with the certainty of a scientist
who has tested them before he talked about them. He has
the certainty of one who has run and raced since the
Eisenhower presidency, won national championships when
Johnson was in office, and ran for 24 straight hours after
Carter was elected.

Tom Osler has tried about everything in running, and he
knows what grows when the right seeds are planted.

— *Joe Henderson*

PREFACE

This book is a guide to training and racing for the competitive distance runner. While I have been trained in the rigors of scientific thinking, what I present here is a kind of craftsmanship, not science. I have distilled my experience as a competitive runner over the past 23 years. I have studied what others have written and said, but more importantly I have tried to watch closely the effects of various training methods on myself and my friends who run with me.

The success of the East Germans in the 1976 Olympic Games has called attention to the supposed advantages of employing technology to assist in the training of runners. I say bunk! The joys of running alone in the forest will never be replaced by the laboratory, nor will the inspiration of a truly charismatic coach ever be replaced by the man in white taking blood samples. Yes, the East Germans were successful in many sports, but so were the Africans who were forced to train under the most primitive conditions.

Science is wonderful (as a mathematician, I am one of her servants myself), but she has her limitations. Frankly, I believe running is far too complicated for successful technical analysis at this time. It is the runners themselves, through their direct empirical findings, who will point the way for the professional physiologist and rarely, very rarely, that the physiologist will provide practical knowledge of use to the competing athlete. In the words of the great mathematician and engineer Oliver Heaviside, "One does not need to understand the physiology of digestion in order to enjoy a good meal."

There are many today who attribute special health benefits to running. Indeed, there are medical professionals who even claim that completion of a marathon grants the runner a certain number of years insurance against heart failure. Again, I say bunk!

Marathon racing is a very specialized and very difficult sport. I have watched men crawl and stagger through the final miles of a marathon under the delusion that they were doing their bodies a favor. I love running, but I do not wish to be numbered with those who make claims of special life-extending benefits from it.

People who find their lives rich with interesting and absorbing activities often enjoy better health than those who find life dull. The reader may wish to believe that running will greatly improve his health or even extend his life. Perhaps it will, but I wish to say that there is nothing in my experience that indicates this. Indeed, I have often witnessed that severe strains which competitive long-distance racing places on the body can have a very negative effect. Moderate running does make one feel better, as does moderate activity of many other types, but the extremes of racing are anything but healthy. One goal of this book is to awaken the reader to the methods of reducing the damaging effects of running and increasing the health-giving benefits.

More than 10 years ago, I wrote a small booklet entitled *The Conditioning of Distance Runners*. I was surprised that so many runners found its contents helpful in improving their performances. In this book, I have updated those ideas, based on my most recent experience, and have added considerable new material detailing the concerns of one who races. The chapters on diet, weather, shoes, along with details of how to race every distance from three to 100 miles are all new.

Before taking advice, the reader should ask where the advice originated. The ideas presented in this book evolved from my long career in which I have run in more than 750 races, ranging from 880 yards to more than 100 miles, and have covered 50,000-plus miles in training.

I was given the name "Turtle" early in my career because of my slow basic speed; I had never run 100 yards faster than 14 seconds or the quarter-mile in under 64 seconds. In spite of this speed handicap, my love for running ultimately brought modest racing success. I won the National AAU 25-Kilometer Championship in 1964 and the 30-Kilometer Championship in 1967. In 1967, I won the National RRC 50-Mile title and ran my best marathon with 2:29:04 at Boston, placing 19th. That same year, I was fourth in the National AAU Marathon at Holyoke, Mass. More recently, I completed a 24-hour run, covering 114 miles.

ACKNOWLEDGMENTS

The methods recommended in this book owe their existence to my good fortune in gleaning the personal experience of the many coaches and runners with whom I have trained and raced. In my earliest years, these included Browning Ross, two-time Olympian and founder of the Road Runners Club of America; the late Dr. William Ruthrauff, an insatiable student of all aspects of running, and Jack Barry, champion marathoner and inventive genius. I feel a warm and extraordinary indebtedness to Ed Dodd who has not only been a lifetime companion of the road, but an indefatigable colleague in search of the lost history of this sport. If Olympic gold medals were awarded for sheer guts and love of sport, the above four men would have a bag full.

Tribute must also be given to one man whom I have never met, Arthur Lydiard of New Zealand. Marathoner, coach of Olympic champions, author and lecturer, the stamp of his influence is evident throughout much of this book.

Special thanks go to Joe Burke, Dr. Larry Delaney, Joe Henderson, Jeff Heppard, Eric Johnson, Dr. Gabe Mirkin, Dr. George Sheehan, Ben Trimble, Dr. Joanne Trimble and Bob Zazzali for reading my original manuscript and offering many suggestions for improvement. Finally, my thanks to Bob Anderson and his staff at World Publications.

PART ONE
Training Smartly

1

METHODS AND
THEIR USES

1. Isn't long-distance running a natural sport?

One must distinguish between running a long distance at
an easy gait simply as a means of travel and the modern
sport of racing the distance as fast as one can possibly go.

Indeed, the human body was designed to cover great
distances on foot. Look at man and you see that about
one-half his body weight is comprised of his powerful leg
muscles. These he can use to cover great distances with
relatively little strain by walking, and perhaps walking and
slow running. He is even superior to the horse at these
labors when the distance exceeds 100 miles. So yes, easy
running and walking for great distances are natural to man
and quite healthful.

However, long-distance *racing* is a modern "perver-
sion." It is certainly not natural. To race great distances as
fast as possible places a far greater strain on the tendons
and muscles of the feet and legs than they were designed
to withstand. Long-distance racing is a very specialized
sport requiring considerable training before the body is
conditioned to execute it well.

2. Isn't long-distance running healthy?

It can be argued easily that more people have died from a

lack of exercise than *ever* expired from too much. However, one must be careful of the extremes.

The person who runs an easy hour, five days each week, will never be a champion runner, but he will enjoy far more robust health than he would if he simply spent his time watching TV.

However, the champion runner has passed through the phase of good health on the difficult road to athletic fitness. In particular, racing long distances places far greater strain on the body than it can respond to in a healthy fashion. It does, in fact, weaken the runner and make him more susceptible to injury and illness than does "running for fun."

3. If long-distance racing is unnatural and self-abusive, why do you do it?

Why do people climb mountains? Why do they take up boxing? These sports clearly are dangerous. I like to race, and 23 years and 750 races have taught me how to defend myself against the dangers inherent in the sport.

I am kind to myself in racing and rarely go all-out. In this way, I manage to minimize injuries. In spite of my precautions, an occasional race will lower my resistance and bring on a cold or tendon inflammation. Nevertheless, I am far healthier as a racer than I would be if I didn't exercise at all.

4. If long-distance racing is, to a degree, damaging to one's health, what safety precautions should the runner observe?

There are many specific precautions the runner should heed, and these will be taken up in detail at the appropriate time in this book. For now, it suffices to observe that *injury is the runner's shadow.* Injury follows him with *every* step he takes.

Thus, any sane training program must place injury-prevention as the number-one consideration. Every training alteration must be considered in the light of its potential for doing tendon or muscle damage. It does the runner no good to be in the best shape of his life if every step hurts so badly that he can't even start a race.

Few runners think, "Will more mileage hurt my tendons?" "Will faster quarters injure my knees?" As a result, many are plagued with injury. Look at any high school or college cross-country team. How many of the runners complete the season without injury? Probably less than half, and these are young athletes who enjoy the healing powers of youth.

5. What are the various types of running from which a training program can be designed?

For the sake of simplicity, we shall consider only five basic training elements:
1. Walking;
2. Running mixed with walking;
3. Long, slow, continuous runs;
4. Interval speed runs;
5. Fast, long, continuous runs.

I'll now answer questions on the positive and negative effects of each of these five.

6. Is walking useful as a training tool for the competitive runner?

By walking, I mean ordinary brisk walking at a speed of from 3-4 miles per hour. I do not mean "heel and toe" race walking which isn't really a walk at all but is a stiff-legged run. In the past, walking was considered to be an integral part of the runner's training program. This is no longer true for most runners, and they suffer because of it.

Good effects: Brisk walking is probably the most natural exercise for man. As a tool for promoting good circulation and overall robust health, it is unmatched. Yes, it is even better than running because walking does not place a heavy strain on the tendons of the foot and leg. Walkers endure far fewer injuries than runners. For the competitive runner, walking is marvelous restorative exercise. It is like a gentle massage. Brisk walking can be used in the evening as a means of promoting circulation to all parts of the legs without straining them. It promotes the healing of inflamed tendons and hastens the removal of the products of fatigue generated earlier in the day by hard running.

Bad effects: As far as one's general health is concerned, there are no bad effects from walking. However, walking is not vigorous enough to train the body for hard racing. I know people who can backpack all day but would be hard-pressed to run five miles at the slowest speed.

7. What about running mixed with walking?

A suitable mixture of running and walking can allow a person to cover enormous distances with relatively little fatigue. For example, a well-trained runner might cover 40 miles in training by alternately running two miles in 15 minutes, then walking a quarter-mile in four minutes. Continuing in this way—running two miles, then walking a quarter—he can complete the 40 miles with far less fatigue than if he had tried to run the entire distance. Very few runners use this training technique today. This is unfortunate.

Good effects: By mixing walking with slow running, one can keep the circulatory system active for a long period of time without placing so much strain on the tendons. Thus, a firm foundation (base) for endurance activities is established. Also, the walking promotes the removal of the waste products of fatigue caused by the running.

Bad effects: While the heart and lungs are stimulated by this activity, the pace is so slow that it does little to prepare the runner's coordination for the fast pace of racing. Also, one cannot stop and walk in any but the very long races without completely "blowing" one's performance.

Another difficulty is that it takes longer to complete a workout in this manner. By running continuously, you might get a superior training effect in a shorter time.

8. Isn't long, slow, continuous running the best way to build foundation for racing?

Perhaps, but a mixture of running and walking is also very effective if one has the time necessary to do it. Long, slow running is probably the most popular form of training used by marathon runners today.

Good effects: Conditions the cardio-respiratory system and thereby develops the runner's base. The slow pace is less likely to injure tendons and muscles than is faster running.

Bad effects: It does not teach the runner to relax at the fast pace needed for racing. It does little to develop the specific abilities needed for racing. It does little to develop the specific abilities needed for racing (sharpening). In spite of the slow pace used, long runs can leave the tendons sore simply because of the long time the runner is on his feet. Unlike running mixed with walking, the waste products of fatigue are not removed as quickly.

9. What is interval speed running? What are its effects?

Here, the runner runs a short distance very rapidly and many times during the workout. Between fast runs, he rests, walks or runs slowly. Usually, the fast runs are at better than race pace. For example, a four-minute miler might run 10 fast quarters in 58 seconds. Between the fast quarters, he recovers by running a quarter in two minutes.

This form of training is called "interval training" when done on a track with the fast and slow segments timed. It is called "fartlek" when done on trails in the woods where both the distance and time of the various segments are only approximated. During the 1950s most runners trained this way year-round. Some great runners still do.

Good effects: Because of the fast pace used, the runner learns to relax well at racing speed; it develops efficiency of movement. These workouts often last 1-2 hours in the case of well-trained runners, and thus they also have a strong effect on the circulatory system.

Bad effects: The fast pace makes tendon and muscle damage more likely. Also, runners tend to be very competitive in these workouts. In this way, they utilize valuable endocrine "juices" that should be saved for hard racing.

Many a runner has left his race on the training circuit by being too competitive in his interval workouts.

10. What are the effects of fast, continuous runs?

This is the hardest form of training. It is almost as difficult as racing itself. Here, the runner selects a distance, usually 5-15 miles, and runs it in training—at a pace which is close to his racing effort.

Good effects: The fast pace teaches the runner to relax at racing speed. The runner can also learn pace judgment, since he is closely approximating racing conditions.

Bad effects: These workouts induce considerable fatigue. Fatigue is the seed from which injury is born. Also, runners often race each other or they watch during these workouts. This depletes the precious store of nervous energy which he should jealously preserve for racing.

11. Looking back over these five methods of training, it would appear that interval speed running should produce the quickest results. Is this true?

Yes, over the short term, but not over the long term. Because interval speed running affects all three physiological components—cardio-respiratory, neuro-muscular and psycho-endocrine—it can give the runner his best performance possible if only a few months are available for training.

However, over a period of many years, it is best to build a foundation solidly with slower methods first. In this way, the runner develops a solid foundation from which to launch better and better races when sharpening training is incorporated. These methods are the subject in the next three chapters.

2
BASE AND SHARPENING WORK

12. What is the source of modern training concepts?

Present training theory is largely the result of the cumulative experience of distance runners over at least the past 150 years. Little practical knowledge has been gained from physiologists working in laboratories, although their important work continues vigorously today.

One man is responsible for clearly formulating and teaching the concepts which today dominate training practice. He is the great New Zealand coach Arthur Lydiard who became famous in 1960 through the Olympic gold-medal performances of his pupils Peter Snell and Murray Halberg.

13. In a nutshell, what are Lydiard's main ideas?

Lydiard observed that athletes cannot maintain peak racing form year-round. Even if one uses the same training methods each month, there will be periods when performance is high and other times, for seemingly no reason related to training, when the runner is in a slump.

Next, Lydiard teaches the runner to select a few races during the year in which he wants to do his best and be reasonably sure of reaching peak racing form at this time.

During most of the year, the runners train at a relatively

slow pace for long distances. This is a form of rest for the nervous system during which the circulatory system becomes very efficient. About two months prior to when the runner wishes to peak, he shifts to shorter and faster training in order to add efficiency of muscular movement to the strong base of endurance that was developed previously. He thus "sharpens" for races.

Lydiard's ideas have been very much misunderstood in spite of their simplicity.

14. In what way has Lydiard been misunderstood?

Much attention has been focused on long, slow distance (LSD) runs which Lydiard advocated for base training. Running publications have featured hundreds of articles during the past 10 years espousing the merits of easy, relaxed training. This is good.

However, for those who wish to race well, the concept of peaking at certain critical times must also be understood. Running literature has largely ignored this essential fact. Lydiard did *not* reject fast training methods. Lydiard's runners did more fast running than their competitors, at the appropriate time of the year. These athletes drew on the reserves of a strong base that they previously developed through endurance running.

15. Is your book largely an exposition of Lydiard's training ideas?

No. Over the past 23 years, I have studied every available work on distance running. My running companions and I have experimented with most of the training ideas that were fashionable. This experience has led us to believe that Lydiard has provided the best general view of the sport. Nevertheless, there are probably many specific recommendations offered in this book with which Lydiard would disagree.

16. What is "base training"? What is "sharpening"?

It is convenient to imagine that a runner's performance is the result of two aspects of his conditioning: his base training and his sharpening training.

The runner's *base level* is the result of his inherited endurance and his years of endurance-related activities. These could include walking, cycling, swimming, cross-country skiing, basketball, running and other activities. These do not produce specific neuromuscular efficiency for a specific running event but do add to overall endurance.

Runners often use long runs, at a pace far slower than race speed, in order to elevate their base level. Physiologically speaking, base training conditions the heart and lungs (cardio-respiratory system) which are the primary organs used by the distance runner.

The runner's *sharpened level* is the result of very specific training for his event. If he is a four-minute miler, he must run many quarter-miles in 60 seconds in order to master relaxation and efficiency at this speed. The muscles must learn not to oppose one another (tie up) but to relax completely until needed. The stride must be as smooth and efficient as possible. All this is obtained through neuro-muscular efficiency.

In addition, successful racing calls into play the psycho-endocrine system. The stimulation of competition causes "juices" (hormones) to flow within the runner's blood to produce times that would be impossible to achieve during non-racing conditions.

In summary, then, base training conditions the cardio-respiratory system; runners most often use long, slow runs to develop their base. Sharpening training affects both the neuro-muscular system and the psycho-endocrine system; it is achieved physically by fast running at race pace and psychologically through charismatic coaching, self-motivation and related methods.

17. Give an actual example of the difference between base and sharpened levels of performance.

In the summer of 1965, I had been training exclusively with base methods. For more than two years, my training had consisted of 75 miles per week of steady running at about 7:30 per mile. I was pleased with my racing performances which included 10 miles in 56 minutes. I saw no reason to increase my training speed, since I was racing faster than ever and enjoying my training as never before. Besides, faster training always increases the chance for injury.

Then, one day I was dramatically shaken. A younger runner whom I had advised and trained for a few years beat me two weeks in a row at six miles on the track. He had never beaten me previously, and for some crazy personal reason I lay awake at night, unable to sleep, concerned about these defeats. I decided to try faster training methods—interval half-miles at a fast pace.

Six weeks later, at the National AAU One-Hour Run Championship (Eastern Section), I was a new runner. It was a hot humid night in Falls Church, Va., yet I won passing 10 miles in 53:03, some three minutes faster than my previous best.

This example illustrates the effects of all three physiological systems mentioned previously:

1. The *cardio-respiratory* system had been conditioned for two years with long, slow runs at 7:30 pace. My base training resulted in 56:00 for 10 miles.

2. *Neuro-muscular* efficiency was achieved by the addition of fast half-mile spurts.

3. The *psycho-endocrine* system was activated by the intense feeling of despair at being beaten by my student. Worry and sleepless nights combined to activate juices that allowed me to run far faster than ever before in just six weeks.

In short, the neuro-muscular and psycho-endocrine systems had been activated to produce a sharpened level. I subsequently improved all my times in races, since my average speed increased by about 20 seconds per mile.

18. Having "peaked" through sharpening training, how long can the runner continue racing fast?

Not too long. In general, it takes about 4-6 weeks from the time the runner begins sharpening training to when he reaches his peak. After that, he can maintain the peak (with some luck) for another 4-6 weeks at the most. After hitting the peak, his performances begin to deteriorate and eventually he must return to his base level.

19. Why can't the runner maintain his peak level indefinitely?

Nature demands a price for all this fast racing. The athlete has only so much reserve energy. The peak racing level has been achieved at the price of the runner's basic health.

The psycho-endocrine system, which played a principal role in elevating the runner's racing times to peak level, is a *reserve system.* The body intends it to be used only for emergency purposes. Its use, in fact, shocks the entire body in a destructive way, causing the runner to become more susceptible to illness and injury. While he might foolishly wish to drive his body on toward personal best racing performances, nature—being far wiser— automatically turns the system off. In so doing, she protects the body from excessive damage and initiates a new *rest phase* which athletes commonly call a slump.

To illustrate the dangerous effects of peaking, consider the story of a small woman who ran from the house at the sound of her husband's cries. While he worked under the family car, the jack had slipped, and he was pinned under the vehicle. This woman, who ordinarily could not lift a heavy suitcase, grasped the bumper and lifted the car just high enough for her husband to slide free. Her psycho- endocrine system had momentarily made her into a super-woman—but at what price? She suffered permanent back damage. Her skeletal system was not designed for such Herculean efforts even though, when necessity de- manded, she could produce them.

In the same way, the runner who has peaked finds himself in a frail state. His resistance to colds is very much lowered. Faster racing puts additional strain on his over- worked tendons and muscles. Is it any wonder that so many runners suffer bone fractures, tendon inflammation, mononucleosis, etc. upon reaching the pinnacle of their racing performances?

If the runner isn't wise enough deliberately to reduce his racing and training soon after he reaches his peak, then nature will do it for him. She will retaliate by inflicting injury or illness, forcing the runner off the track in despair.

20. What, then, is the overall training method recommended here?

The cardio-respiratory system is the most important component of the distance runner's physiology. It determines his base level, which is capable of slow, continual development over a period of many years.

Thus, the runner should do base training, consisting of long, slow runs and walks for most of the year. He should select one brief period, or perhaps two, per year during which he wishes to race at his best. During this time, he peaks by using faster methods of training. After two (or at most three) months of fast training and racing, he returns to slow running so as not to induce a severe slump from the exhausting effects of utilizing his psycho-endocrine reserves.

To illustrate these ideas, consider a runner who in 1978 runs two miles in 11 minutes on base training only. Figure One shows how his base level slowly improves so that in two years he can race two miles in 10 minutes.

Now, suppose the same two-miler periodically incorporates sharpening training. His base level remains unchanged as shown in Figure Two (dashed line), but his actual performance illustrates peaks and slumps (solid line). At "A," he begins sharpening training at which point he can run his two-mile race in 10:55. Six weeks later, he reaches his peak at "B," where he runs 10:25. Another hard month of racing and training brings him to "C," where his body has reached the point of exhaustion due to these unusually hard efforts. Rather than deliberately easing off his training and racing when the first signs of the slump occur, our inexperienced runner continues thrashing out hard runs. The result is that, in a week or two, his performance level crashes to the discouraging low at "D," where he races below base level, running 11:00.

Gradually, he recovers and by 1979, seven months later, he is ready to peak again. He begins speed training as before and reaches a new high plateau as shown in "E," "F," and "G." Once again his body is exhausted from so much hard racing and training, and a new slump is

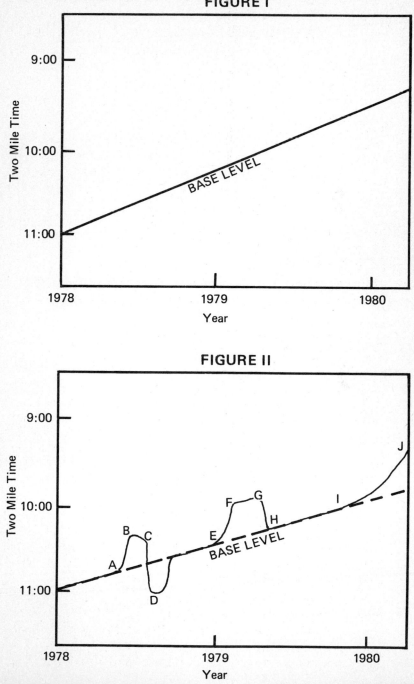

FIGURE I

FIGURE II

about to begin at "G." However, our runner has learned from the precipitous decline of the past year ("C" to "D"). He now very wisely eliminates all forms of speed training and returns once again to slow base-training methods. As a result, his performance level does not drop rapidly but only slowly returns to his base level as shown from "G" to "H."

In summary, then, it is recommended that the runner select a period of about six weeks during the year when he wishes to race at his very best. During the remainder of the year, he uses slow-base training methods and races with a casual attitude. Faster training methods initiate the sharpening period and result in peak performances in about 4-6 weeks. The peak can then be maintained for about 4-6 weeks with due care. Any unusual strain at this time could abruptly terminate the peak and bring the performance level crashing down below the base level.

21. Can a runner's performance level really come crashing down overnight due to excessive stress?

Yes, indeed! In 1968, the Olympic Games were held in Mexico City at high altitude. In order to condition the best American marathoners, the AAU arranged a high-altitude training camp at Alamosa, Colo. Regional trial races were staged throughout the country in late 1967, and the winners were given expenses for this training camp.

The Atlantic City Marathon was designated as such a trial, and I eagerly wanted to win it. I had earlier in the year finished fourth in the National AAU Marathon Championship, as well as winning the AAU 30-Kilometer Championship. I felt ready for a good marathon.

The trial was set for Oct. 20, 1967, and I began sharpening training in early September. Each week, I felt myself running faster and stronger as the seemingly magical effects of the sharpening process brought smoothness and efficiency to my stride.

In late September, a 16-mile relay race is annually staged in Atlantic City. Four members each run four miles. I was not on a team, but decided to drive to Atlantic City and run the first four miles of the race as a speed workout.

This race is dominated by college teams, and I found myself easily in the lead as I neared the finish of the four-mile leg. Feeling good, I decided to run the second leg also. Well, I ran the second four miles, and then the third. At 12 miles, I still had the lead over all the relay teams, but now I was badly tired. Nevertheless, I decided to run the last four miles.

How foolish! My legs could easily have handled a 16-mile race had I started at 16-mile pace. I had, however, started at four-mile pace! Exhausted, I was passed by two relay teams in the final two miles of the race. I had run the hardest 16 miles of my life for nothing. The next several weeks, my weary legs dragged through each workout. Gone was the feeling of strength and leg-life which I had enjoyed before the relay. I had abruptly terminated the sharpening process in less than two hours of running and brought my performance level down even below the base.

When the big trial marathon came one month later, I finished a washed-out fourth.

22. Don't most good distance runners remain in racing form year-round?

Everything is relative. Today, good distance runners train 100 miles per week and more year-round, and thus can give credible racing performances at almost any distance from the mile to the marathon at any time.

However, there are so many good runners today that even a slight improvement in one's racing speed is likely to result in a major improvement in one's finishing position. The sharpening techniques advocated in this book generally result in an improvement of from 10-20 seconds per mile in racing speed, assuming the runner was at base level when the sharpening process began.

23. Don't most good runners use some form of speed training several days each week year-round?

Yes, this is probably true. As mentioned earlier, Lydiard's concept of peaking for major races has never gained complete acceptance. Runners still cherish the dream that they can stay in peak racing form for 12 months of the year. When they try this, they find that their performance level is unpredictable. They, too, have mild peaks and slumps. But unlike the runners who plan for peak periods, they don't really know when they will come.

Also, unless the body is allowed to rest for most of the year by using slow base training, it will not have that store of energy which can be exploded at the right time to bring about a high peak level of performance.

In short, runners who use speed work all year long have peaks, but they are smaller than they would be had they enjoyed more rest.

24. Most runners, then, use essentially the same training year-round, while others change from slow to faster methods to produce sharpening peaks. Can you cite actual examples?

In recent years, two great runners illustrated the results of using the two systems, Ron Clarke and Lasse Viren.

Clarke, of Australia, held the world record for nearly every distance between two miles and 10 miles during the 1960s. In his book *The Unforgiving Minute,* he reveals that he tried to stay in top form year-round. Clarke always ran well, but he was never at his very best in major championships. Olympic and Commonwealth Games titles went to lesser athletes, while Clarke placed third and fourth. The men who beat him frequently could not hope to touch his world records, yet they had managed to peak on the right day.

Apparently, Clarke made the mistake of ignoring a basic principle in modern running: Unless you plan for your peaks, they will come unexpectedly—most often at the wrong times in insignificant races.

Viren, the great Finnish runner, amazed the world by winning both the 5,000 and 10,000-meter races in the 1972 and '76 Olympic Games. Yet Viren was beaten again and again at other times. For example, he finished third in the European Championships at 5000 meters in 1974. Why was Viren invincible in the Olympics but thoroughly mortal at other times?

Many accused him of practicing some secret blood transfusion technique which supposedly gave him greater oxygen-carrying capacity. But these are the excuses invented by those who could not believe the improvement that Viren could make through sharpening. The Finnish coaches had enjoyed an extensive visit by Arthur Lydiard prior to the 1972 Olympic Games. Lydiard taught them his methods of preparing a runner for maximum performance at the right time.

Viren became another example of the success that Lydiard's methods could bring. Peter Snell had demonstrated the effectiveness of peaking back in the 1960 and '64 Olympic Games, and no one accused him of "blood-doping." Snell had trouble breaking four minutes for the mile a few months prior to the Tokyo Olympics, and many thought he was washed up. Yet after a few weeks of sharpening, Snell won gold medals at 800 and 1500 meters, and what's more, won them decisively.

3

PLANNING A BASE SCHEDULE

25. What is the essential character of base training?

During base training, effort is made to develop the cardio-respiratory system so as to increase the overall endurance and heartiness of the runner. At the same time, it is essential to maintain a relaxed and non-competitive atmosphere so as not to activate the psycho-endocrine system and thereby burn up the runner's nervous energy.

Remember that the cardio-respiratory system is capable of continuous improvement, whereas the runner has only limited supplies of endocrine juices which can be utilized to provide the needed "extra" in racing. Runners who insist on racing each other in every workout will find themselves feeling flat when the big races arrive.

26. When should the runner begin base training?

Anytime. Since base training conditions the circulatory system, it can be recommended as a health-generating activity for almost anyone. In general, it does not put excessive strain on the muscles and tendons of the feet and legs because of the relatively slow pace used and the need to terminate all workouts while the runner is still fresh.

If the runner has been doing sharpening training and has

experienced his peak, he should return to base training as soon as he notices his performances deteriorating. As mentioned before, this will happen about 4-6 weeks after the peak is reached. By returning to base work soon enough, he will enjoy racing at a relatively high level for several months more. If he does not return to base training in sufficient time, he will drop very quickly into a severe slump. Illness and injury frequently will follow.

27. How long should base training continue?

Base training should continue for at least six months and preferably one year before sharpening training begins. Time is required to develop the base. If the runner has just enjoyed the success of peak racing, time will be needed for his nervous energy to regenerate itself. This can take place during base training because of the casual nature of the work.

In some cases, runners elect to do only base training and never sharpen. This makes sense when general health is considered, for base training has little of the negative effects created by sharpening. Also, many runners simply don't like to run fast. For them, base training is all they desire from the sport, and they are satisfied with their level of racing performance.

However, should the runner wish to realize his full racing potential, sharpening training must ultimately be undertaken.

28. Is it best to run the same mileage every day?

Absolutely not! There should be frequent days for rest during which the runner does very little work, followed by days of heavier training. If he wished to run 70 miles per week, it would be unwise to run 10 miles on each day of the week.

29. How, then, should the mileage be distributed over a typical week during base training?

There are several possibilities, one of which is:

Day		Length	Distance run
Monday	*Thur*	Short	5% of week's total
Tuesday	*Fri*	Medium	15% of week's total
Wednesday	*Sa*	Long	30% of week's total
Thursday	*Sun*	Short	5% of week's total
Friday	*Mon*	Medium	15% of week's total
Saturday	*Tue*	Medium or short	10% of week's total
Sunday	*Wed*	Time trial or race	10% of week's total

Note: Percentages are approximate; add small amounts needed to total 100%.

Some runners choose to make every other day an easy day. Thus, the pattern becomes hard day, easy day, hard day, easy day. . . . This is also very effective.

30. Do you really need all those easy days? Won't you become a better runner by working hard every day?

Rest is as important as stress when building a runner's base. Each workout tears the body down a bit. Ideally, the runner should recover overnight, but often this is not the case. The easy days are a safety valve, allowing the body to recover and make itself stronger. Without the easy days, the runner is likely to stagnate and improve little. Even worse, he may break down with injury or illness.

31. Can I use walking mixed with running rather than a continuous run?

Yes, if continuous running seems too hard. A runner in fairly good condition might want to run continuously at a steady speed and reserve walking mixed with running for those days when he feels a bit bushed. For the novice, walking might be necessary in most workouts.

I find it convenient to walk briskly for five minutes, following every 20 minutes of running. More walking seems to leave my legs heavy and unwilling to run again. Be sure to walk with vigor, as it is necessary to keep the circulation moving. Don't stroll as you would at a shopping mall. A slow walk does the legs harm, as the blood is not forced back to the heart through the capillaries. For me, walking at about 3½ miles per hour is appropriate, but this is an individual matter.

32. How fast should one run in these workouts?

With the exception of the time-trial or race, all these runs should be at a comfortable, relaxed pace. Certainly one should not be running so fast that continuous conversation is difficult.

The terms "slow" and "fast" are relative. For a world-class marathoner (who can run 26 consecutive five-minute miles) six minutes per mile is an easy relaxed speed. For most runners, a pace somewhere between seven and eight minutes per mile should be used in base training.

For a particular runner, 7:30 pace might be quite comfortable today, but tomorrow, when he is tired, 9:00 pace might be appropriate. Do not worry about the actual pace as recorded by the watch. Rather, judge the appropriate pace by how you feel. Never run yourself to exhaustion.

33. How should one feel at the end of the workout?

You should feel as though you could turn around and complete the entire workout again if demanded. In short, on any given day you should only do half of what you really feel capable. In this way, sufficient energy is held in reserve in order to build and improve. Runners who kill themselves every day do not improve as rapidly as those who hold something in reserve.

The one exception to this is the time-trial or race which will be somewhat more exhausting.

34. What is the ideal length for the race or time-trial?

The longer the race, the greater the degree of fatigue created, all other things being equal. Thus, if the race is too long, it will take more than one day for complete recovery. I like two or three miles for my races and time trials. I can recover in a few hours from an all-out three-mile run, while an all-out 10-miler takes almost one week.

The runner should put some effort into these trials and races, but he should be careful not to overdo it. Remember, it is best to keep a casual attitude toward competition during base training. The time to utilize one's nervous energy will come later when sharpening training is employed.

35. What purpose is served by the weekly race or time-trial during the base-building phase?

The training pace has been very slow. These trials help to remind the runner of the fast pace needed in racing and, more importantly, of the need to practice relaxation while running at all times. Often, runners become quite inefficient in their movements from slow running. The trial is an opportunity to strive for smoothness and relaxation while moving fast.

These trials also help to maintain some measure of good coordination at a fast running speed. Without them, the runner might not be able to reach a peak after just six weeks of sharpening training.

36. Is it best to run actual races or is it better to run time-trials?

There are advantages and disadvantages to both. When racing, one learns to keep one's head during the usual overly-fast start. One learns the elements of racing tactics and pacing while running in the midst of a crowd. The major drawback of racing at this stage of the runner's training is that he is likely to pump himself full of those endocrine juices that he should be preserving. It isn't easy to maintain a casual attitude when the starting gun is fired.

The advantage of solo time-trials is that you can select the distance and type of terrain you will use. Also, it is difficult to get excited about these things when you are alone with a watch on the track. The times are almost always a good deal slower in time-trials than they would be in races, because one does not have an adrenalin build-up. This, however, is good during base training. For example, a runner capable of 10:30 for two miles in a race might only do 11:00 in a time-trial since he simply can't get all that "psyched."

37. What is the purpose of running one long run each week?

The long run helps to stimulate the circulatory system. It also gives the runner experience at staying on his feet for an extended period of time. This is a valuable psychological experience. Later, in racing when it might seem impossible to finish as fatigue progresses, the runner can think back on these training runs of great length and gather confidence from them. Also, these help show the runner where his endurance limits end.

Eventually, most runners want to try the marathon and perhaps ultimately the ultra-marathons. For these events, it is best to have a background of many very long, slow training runs.

The best reason of all, however, is that they are so much fun. For example, I enjoy nothing better than leaving my home at 6 a.m. in the summer, and gently running and walking to the seashore—a distance of about 50 miles. I arrive at the beach at about 2 p.m., fresh and ready for a nice swim. My wife and children (who have come by car) then relax with me, enjoy a walk on the boardwalk and a delicious seafood dinner.

38. Is a mixture of running and walking always used on the long runs?

Not always. I can run up to about 25 miles comfortably at a speed of about 8:30 per mile (when I feel good) at a continuous pace. However, when I feel a bit bushed or am running much farther, I like to mix walking with the running so as not to be overly tired at the end.

39. I wish to start base training. How many miles should I run during the first week?

This depends on how much training you have been doing. Suppose you have been running about 35 miles per week over the past few months. It's a good idea to reduce this by 10% so as not to overdo it. Thus, the runner will do about 31 miles during the first week of base training. Using the schedule mentioned earlier, this gives the following daily mileages:

Monday	about 5% of 31 miles	equals 2 miles
Tuesday	about 15% of 31 miles	equals 5 miles
Wednesday	about 30% of 31 miles	equals 9 miles
Thursday	about 5% of 31 miles	equals 2 miles
Friday	about 15% of 31 miles	equals 5 miles
Saturday	about 10% of 31 miles	equals 3 miles
Sunday	time trial at	4 miles
		Total equals 30 miles

40. Why is it important to begin with a relatively low mileage?

Because the weekly mileage will be slowly and gradually increased over the next several months. In this way, the circulatory system will be taught to respond to greater and greater demands of long running. If the initial mileage is too great, the runner will not develop as the mileage increases but will break down from the excessive strain encountered.

41. How should the weekly training load be increased?

The easy runs, the medium runs and the long runs are best increased at different rates. I recommend the following:

Easy runs . . . . not increased in length
Medium runs . . . . increased in length by one mile every two or three weeks
Long runs . . . . increased by one mile each week until about 22-25 miles is reached

42. These increases don't seem all that hard. What would the training schedule look like 12 weeks later?

First glances can be deceiving. After 12 weeks of following the recommended increases, the runner will have nearly doubled his weekly mileage. The schedule then looks like:

l to r, Frank Bozanich (first), John Garlepp (second) and Joe Burns during the early miles. (Photo by Ed Dodd)

	Initial	After 12 weeks
Monday	2 miles	2 miles
Tuesday	5 miles	10 miles
Wednesday	9 miles	21 miles
Thursday	2 miles	2 miles
Friday	5 miles	10 miles
Saturday	4 miles	8 miles
Sunday	4 miles	6 miles
Totals	**31 miles**	**59 miles**

43. That is indeed quite an increase! Can the runner continue increasing his weekly mileage at this rate?

Probably not. Once the weekly mileage has doubled, he should experiment with more gradual increases. The runner's actual response to the training is always the best guide. If he is fresh and feels good, then a greater load can probably be tolerated. However, if he seems tired and is losing interest in running, a decrease could be called for.

44. Is it necessary to follow the schedule religiously?

Absolutely not! No schedule, however well designed, can anticipate how you will feel on a given day. The schedules outlined previously were only intended to be general guides. Perhaps the weather is fine today, and you feel unusually strong; run farther if you like. Some days you are just inexplicably tired; take another easy day. It does the body no good to drive it on when it is not ready and is in need of rest.

45. If I feel tired before running, should I just skip that workout?

The sensation of fatigue prior to running is sometimes deceptive. I prefer to get out and run a few miles first to see how my body really responds to the effort. If I still feel sluggish, I might turn around and run home, calling it quits, or I might try mixing a lot of walking with the running. I have even resorted to walking and running alternate quarter-miles. Quite often, the walking and running combination makes me feel better than not running at all.

46. Do experienced runners always follow a predetermined schedule?

Even if no written schedule has been prepared, most successful runners follow at least some casual mental picture of a schedule.

For example, the runner will check to make sure that he is getting one time-trial and one long run about every seven days. He will usually check the week's total mileage to make sure that there is a sufficient quantity of running.

As far as easy days go, he frequently takes them when he is too busy with business matters or when the weather is poor. The world will not end if a long run is missed now and then, nor will his racing performances suffer.

47. Once a strong base is built with endurance training methods, is it necessary to continue long training in order to maintain it?

A large reduction in training mileage might be accompanied by a swift decline in racing speed, but the runner's general stamina will decline very, very slowly. Once general endurance is built by the methods described here, it can be maintained with relatively little running.

I shall illustrate this with my own running. In recent years, I have grown weary of training in the cold winter, yet I love the warmth of summer. Thus, my training mileage drops to 40-50 miles of slow running during cold months and picks up to 120-160 miles per week in the summer.

Newcomers to the sport with whom I train do not understand how I can tolerate so rapid an increase in workload from spring to summer. They fail to realize that all the miles I have run over the past 23 years have their benefit.

In April 1977, it took all my energy to break three hours for the Penn Relays Marathon. Yet I cruised through the marathon in 2:56 on a hot humid August night during a 50-mile track race in Maryland in which I ran 5:51:13. You can lose the speed quickly, but the stamina remains.

48. Doesn't all this running interfere with one's family life?

I feel especially guilty about time taken away from my children. For this reason, I usually schedule my workouts for times when they are at school or asleep. In the summer, I often train at 3 a.m. since I am frequently awake at that time, and the air is cool and relatively clean.

Some runners minimize the effect of their training on their loved ones by giving the impression that they run very little. The grand master of this art has to be Ted Corbitt. I visited Ted in 1968. He told me that he had been running 30 miles every day for the past month while going to and from work. My mind staggered at the thought of spending so much time out on the road.

Later, Ted's charming wife Ruth prepared lunch for us. I nearly choked when I heard her remark, "Isn't it nice that my Ted gets a little exercise. Other men sit and watch television, and they drink beer. But not my Ted; he gets his little exercise every day."

4
PLANNING A
SHARPENING SCHEDULE

49. When should sharpening training begin?

About six weeks before the first race in which the runner hopes to give his peak performance. Keep in mind that once the peak is reached, this high level of racing performance can easily be terminated. In most cases, the peak is terminated from 4-6 weeks after it is first reached, because the runner's reserves of nervous energy are then depleted.

50. Is it difficult to sharpen to a peak?

Yes, in two ways. First, there is a greater strain placed upon the runner's body. This means that his overall resistance to illness will be lower during this phase. Faster racing will also make tendon damage more likely.

Second, the fine art of rising to a peak is difficult in that great care must be paid to every aspect of the sharpening process; otherwise, a very low peak if not complete failure will result. This contrasts dramatically with base training which is relatively easy to execute with a high probability of success.

51. If I use the sharpening procedure successfully, how much faster will I be racing?

After six weeks of sharpening training, the runner can expect to be racing about 10-20 seconds per mile faster than he was previously. For example, I was able to reduce my 10-mile time from 56:00 to 53:00 and my marathon from 2:40 to 2:29. My two-mile time improved from 10:10 to 9:45.

52. Are there any reasons why one should not start sharpening training?

Even though the runner may have spent many months developing his base, there are still conditions under which sharpening training is best postponed. Unless his overall health is robust when sharpening begins, the process is likely to fail. In particular note that:

1. The runner should have two solid legs free of injury. Any minor injuries are likely to be aggravated by the fast running used in sharpening.

2. The runner should be free of any colds or minor infections. The sharpening process itself lowers his general resistance and might cause a minor infection to grow into a serious problem that has him in bed rather than on the track.

3. The runner should not be nursing a "hangover" from hard racing. For example, it would be unwise for him to run a hard marathon race within a month of the day he plans to begin sharpening. The body cannot be expected to give superior performances when it is crying for rest.

4. The runner should not be overweight but very lean. This is no time to be dieting. Lose weight first, then undertake sharpening.

53. How would a typical week's schedule appear during sharpening training?

Monday	Easy
Tuesday	Relaxation-speed workout
Wednesday	Moderately long easy run
Thursday	Relaxation-speed workout
Friday	Relaxation-speed workout
Saturday	Medium easy run
Sunday	Race or time trial

The easy run and the relaxation-speed workouts should cover about the same mileage as did the easy run and the medium run during base training, respectively. However, the long run (Wednesday) should be shorter than the long runs used in base training. This is because it is necessary to maintain leg freshness. You cannot do speed work with profit when the legs feel a hangover from previous runs. You can shorten the long run to about three-fourths its previous length.

The total week's mileage should also be somewhat less than before. This is needed to compensate for the fatigue generated by the speed runs. About a 10% reduction should suffice.

54. Just what is a "relaxation-speed" workout?

These are the training sessions during which the runner will learn to relax while running at a fast pace. They differ from the usual *speed* workouts commonly seen, in that the emphasis is first on relaxation and second on speed.

Speed without relaxation is useless to the distance runner. Anyone can run a short distance at a fast pace with his fists clenched and every muscle straining. What the distance runner requires is to be able to coast at nearly top speed with unused muscle fibers in a state of complete relaxation while only those necessary to running are working.

55. Describe in detail my first relaxation-speed workout.

During the first week of sharpening the length of this workout will be about the same as the runner's medium runs during the base-building phase. If his previous medium runs required 12 miles, he will still cover a total of about 12 miles. The workout now proceeds as follows:

1. He runs the first three miles at base training speed in order to warm up. For example, he might run at 7:30 per mile.

2. During the fourth mile, he runs about four fast spurts ranging in length from 50-100 yards. These prepare the muscles for the harder running about to commence.

3. During the fifth mile, he does a long build-up for

about 880-1320 yards. (This will be described in detail shortly.)

4. During the sixth mile, he again does four 50-100-yard bursts.

5. In the seventh mile, he does another half-mile build-up.

6. In the eighth mile, he again does four 50-100-yard bursts.

7. In the ninth mile, he does another 880-yard build-up.

8. He completes the workout by running the last three miles at base training pace, with another four 50-100-yard bursts included.

In short, the workout centers around three long build-ups of half- to three-quarters of a mile. Between these, several short spurts of from 50-100 yards are run to maintain leg-life.

56. Should the short burst of 50-100 yards be run at top speed?

It is never necessary for the distance runner to run at his maximum speed. His very fastest sprinting speed cannot be obtained without a certain measure of strain. This is due to the exaggerated movements used by the driving arms and the stride of excessive length.

However, he can run at *nearly* top speed using considerable relaxation. When doing these bursts (and in any fast running for that matter), he should strive for complete relaxation. Speed is always sacrificed on the altar of relaxation.

At first, these bursts will be relatively slow because the runner will find relaxation difficult. However, after a few weeks of sharpening, he will find that he can go nearly all-out at a smooth, relaxed clip.

57. How are the half-mile build-ups run?

In brief, the pace begins slowly and gradually increases until about the 660-yard mark, at which point the runner is going at nearly top speed. After this, the pace is slowly reduced until the half-mile is completed.

Since it is important to understand fully how these build-ups are executed, I'll describe them now in more detail:

1. The pace begins easily (6:30 mile pace, for example). The runner feels smooth and relaxed.

2. At about 50 yards, the pace is increased somewhat. Now, the runner examines every fiber of his body. Any muscle that is tense is made to relax.

3. Another 50-100 yards down the road, the pace is again increased. As always, the runner analyzes himself, feeling where he is tense. The pace is not accelerated until his entire body is relaxed and striding smoothly at this new speed. He thinks gentle thoughts. His feet strike the ground softly. He imagines running on soft pillows. Everything is effortless.

4. Every 50-100 yards, the pace is again increased. At each new step, complete relaxation is obtained before the next acceleration is attempted. Finally, the runner has covered about 660 yards; he is flying at nearly top speed. When done properly, he will have the momentary sensation that he can sprint at top speed forever. He moves with power, grace and efficiency, and feels as though it is effortless.

5. Now, the pace is slowly decelerated. In steps of 50-100 yards each, he slowly reduces his efforts until he is back at base training speed after running about 880 yards.

The diagram on page 52 illustrates approximately the way in which his speed varies during this half-mile run.

58. Is it important to do these build-ups on a track so that the distances can be accurately measured?

Certainly not. I prefer to do them on the open road and give little thought to the accuracy of the distance run. Sometimes, it's about half a mile, but at other times it turns out to be closer to one mile. This is unimportant. Relaxa-

FIGURE III

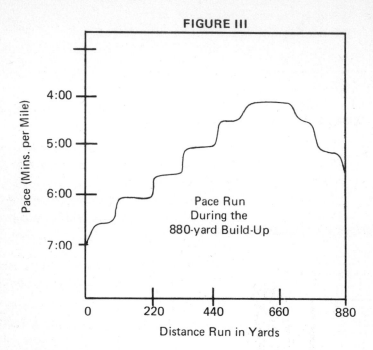

Pace Run
During the
880-yard Build-Up

Distance Run in Yards

tion with speed is the desired goal. Concentrate on an easy, soft, swift stride.

Also, I never time these runs. Timing takes my mind off the need to relax. The worst situation occurs when a coach stands at the edge of the track with his stopwatch, and records the time and distance. In this case, I always tie up from the pressure to produce a fast time.

59. How is the load increased week by week in these relaxation-speed workouts?

The total mileage covered in each workout remains unchanged. For example, if one runs a total of 12 miles for the workout during the first week, it will remain 12 miles each week thereafter.

However, the number of build-ups in each workout increases week by week according to the following plan:

First week	3 x 880 yards
Second week	3 x 880 yards plus 1 x 440 yards
Third week	4 x 880 yards

Fourth week	4 x 880 yards plus 1 x 440 yards
Fifth week	5 x 880 yards
Sixth week	5 x 880 yards plus 1 x 440 yards
Seventh week	6 x 880 yards

60. Your schedule of increases ends after seven weeks. What should I do then?

By this time, you should have reached your peak racing form. You should now consider if further increases in the training load are desirable. I always choose to stop with six 880-yard build-ups and maintain that number through the remaining six weeks, during which I hope to stay at peak racing level.

61. Must I do only 880 yard build-ups? Can't I invent other types of relaxation-speed workouts as well?

Yes, of course. After about four weeks of sharpening training, I usually replace one of the 880-yard build-up workouts with a paced run of about two or three miles. Here, I follow the same build-up procedure used in the 880s, but now the accelerations are less severe, and there is only one speed run in the workout.

Another workout I enjoy is running alternate fast and slow 50-yard spurts for a total distance of two miles. This type of workout tends to accelerate the sharpening process.

62. Besides performing the relaxation-speed workouts, should I be doing anything else to insure success of the sharpening process?

Yes. There is always a chance that the sharpening process will fail. The runner is walking a tightrope. He is at the very edge of his capacity. A little more work, and he might tumble into a deep slump.

This is avoided by paying very careful attention to how the body is reacting both during the workouts and during everyday activities. There are symptoms which point toward probable success of the sharpening technique, and there are symptoms which point toward failure. The runner must learn what these are and be ever watchful. The sharpening process can always be adjusted in response to these signals.

63. What are the symptoms of successful sharpening that I can expect to feel while training?

1. During the first week or two of sharpening, there will be particular difficulty in relaxing during the faster portion of the 880s. However, after 5-7 such workouts, the legs should respond easily and feel relaxed with the continual demands of acceleration. Eventually, the runner should feel as though he could run at top speed indefinitely during the 880s. He should strike the ground softly and feel as though there is not effort from his will-power as his body thirsts to accelerate.

2. A similar experience is noticed during the shorter 50-100-yard bursts. There is no need to command the body; it surges forward of its own will. I repeat that the extremes of sprinting action must be avoided, as this is not needed in distance running. Always use basic distance running form.

3. In the hour following training, the runner should feel a new sensation. Instead of the mild feeling of physical depression which followed the slow workouts, he should feel renewed leg-life and zip. He should have a keen drive to do things and feel a sense of super-awareness of his environment. If this important sensation of vigor is not observed, the fast running is probably too hard, and the sharpening process will likely fail.

64. What signs should I look for in everyday activities which point toward successful sharpening?

1. As the leg muscles strengthen and you master the art of relaxation, many everyday activities become easier. For example, I have observed that when climbing stairs, I seem to rise with no effort at all. This is a feeling I rarely experience during base training.

2. Sometimes you will be unfavorably sensitive to everyday situations which ordinarily did not concern you.

Mild irritability is evident. This is a natural response, as the body is now prepared for action and is ready for the fight.

3. As the body becomes flooded with previously latent energy, a heightened sexual awareness is often evident. When sharpening successfully, I am reminded of the intense sexual drive that I knew as a teenager. This is a natural response, and is one of the surest and most reliable signs that the sharpening process is taking maximum effect.

65. What signs should I look for that point toward failure of the peaking process?

1. Heavy-leggedness and sluggishness following workouts are sure signs that the runner is overdoing it, and probably aiming for too much speed at the price of relaxation.

2. A general "I-don't-care" attitude concerning everyday affairs is characteristic of nervous depletion.

3. The desire to quit during races is a sure sign of having overspent oneself. The body should delight in the battle and thirst for competition.

4. Persistent leg soreness should not be observed.

5. Mild signs of lowered resistance such as headache and sniffles are signs of physical depletion.

66. When I first notice these signs of failure, what action should I take?

You should return to slow running, as during the base building phase, until these negative symptoms disappear. Then, the sharpening process can continue. It will usually only take a day or two before freshness is restored.

Note also that your resistance to illness during this phase of peak racing fitness is not as strong as it was during base training. Just because you can run fast, it does not mean that your overall health is superior. The opposite is true. You are running faster *at the expense of your overall health.* Always keep this in mind and take extra care to avoid drafts, chills, etc.

67. When should I terminate sharpening training?

About three months after the sharpening process began. By this time, the body will probably have used up its reserves, and a return to slow running is now appropriate. Once again, it takes about six weeks of sharpening to build to a peak. The exact length of time that the peak can be sustained will depend on the thoroughness of the runner's base training, on the energy loss due to hard racing and on the care with which he performed the sharpening training.

If the runner's performances begin to slip before three months, then base training should return at once. In this way, he will avoid overly exhausting his reserves, and he will be delighted to observe that his racing performances stay close to peak level and only very slowly return to base level. He can expect to race swiftly for about two months following his return to base training. After about three months, he will have returned to his base level.

68. What will happen if I continue the sharpening process for too long a period?

Your racing performances will decline much more rapidly. The harder you try, the faster you'll fall. Ultimately, sickness or injury will likely overcome you. In this way, nature will see to it that you take the rest she demands.

69. What place has hill training in the sharpening-process?

Arthur Lydiard, in his book *Run to the Top,* recommends that the athlete undergo a period of hill training lasting from 4-6 weeks before beginning fast speed training. For three days of each week, his runners bound up a half-mile hill several times to develop leg strength during this preliminary period.

For most of my life, I have lived in southern New Jersey where there are no real hills. While I never have difficulty racing in areas that are hilly, I've found that when I tried to incorporate Lydiard's hill work into my sharpening training, I became very lethargic. I abandoned the idea, thinking that only very gifted runners possessing far greater strength than I could profit from this work.

In 1970, I moved my family to upstate New York where enormous hills crowd the landscape. It was impossible to escape the hills. For the first eight weeks, my back ached after every workout. (This had only happened previously on the most exhausting runs.) It was impossible to run too slowly.

Finally, after about two months I seemed to adjust to the hills. I could run in any direction, over any changes in elevation, without concern. I lived, trained and raced in this hilly region for two years. I did no sharpening training during this time. I frequently raced two miles on the track in about 10 minutes flat.

When I moved back to the plains of south Jersey, I found that my two-mile times quickly slipped by 30 seconds. I am convinced that running over the hills in training gave me the leg strength and spring necessary to race fast without specifically sharpening. When I returned to flat country, I soon lost this advantage.

This experience has led me to the following conclusion: hill training develops muscular strength and spring. Those who live in hilly regions develop this strength without giving it thought. Runners like myself from level areas must work harder during the sharpening phase. They must do more speed work to develop their full potential.

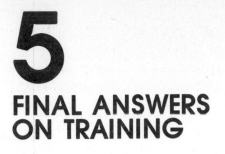

5
FINAL ANSWERS ON TRAINING

70. Where should I train?

One of the remarkable features of distance running is that it can be done almost anywhere. This is in sharp contrast to most other sports. Nevertheless, the serious runner must consider the following:

1. The runner's second worst enemy is the motor vehicle. (His worst enemy is himself, and his tendency to overwork.) Major highways are generally too dangerous for running. Select roads with a *wide,* flat shoulder on which to train. Don't have cars and trucks whizzing past your elbows, inches away.

2. If you can find one, a good trail in the woods can be a wonderful training asset. Ideally, the trail should be free of loose stones and ruts. Look out, however, for hunters and bugs in the warm months.

3. A good track, particularly a cinder track, can provide a fine soft surface free from traffic and dogs. Most runners, however, find it boring to train on athletic fields.

4. When all else fails, a small loop on a grass surface might be available. For example, I have a track which circles my home right inside our fence which measures 16 laps to the mile. My wife uses this frequently, since she has

difficulty with the neighborhood dogs. I sometimes use it for very slow runs and walks.

5. The faster you run, the more critical is the selection of running surface. A smooth, spongy dirt path is best for really hard running.

71. Can training on the open road be safe?

There is always the possibility of being hit. When flesh meets steel, the outcome is certain. There are, however, certain simple training habits which reduce the possibility of tragedy:

1. Always select roads with little traffic and very wide shoulders.

2. Always run on the left side of the road, facing traffic. At least you can jump off the shoulder if a motorist fails to see you.

3. Wear the brightest, most visible colors. Yellow, orange and red might not be the colors you prefer from the standpoint of fashion, but you must make yourself as visible as possible to motorists. Never wear blue, brown or dark gray. I wear such outlandish colors that my neighbors frequently laugh at me. That's great, for then I know I'll be seen and not unexpectedly hit.

4. The situation I fear most on the open road is one vehicle passing another going in my direction. Not only is the passing motorist going at top speed; he perhaps will come up behind me and come within inches of the shoulder on which I'm running. My only hope is that my bright running suit allows him to see me.

5. Finally, the runner's eyes must constantly watch each approaching car. His ears must be alert for vehicles coming from any direction. He must also watch where his feet will fall for holes, glass, stones, etc.

72. Is it wise to train at night?

There absolutely must be enough light for the runner to see stones, holes, bottles, etc., that might be on the running path. A running track with light is perhaps the ideal place for safe evening workouts. Our local college track gets enough stray light from its adjacent parking lots so that I can train there at any hour.

It is very, very dangerous to run on the open road in the dark of night, even if the road is lit. Drivers often don't expect to see pedestrians at night. If you insist on running then, by all means put reflective tape all over your running hat, suit and shoes. I have read of several runners being seriously injured and killed on the road at night, and I will not go out on the highway at night for this reason.

73. Isn't it boring to do long workouts on the track?

Not if you know how. I like to train on our local cinder track, because the surface has more "give" to it than does the hard road. This helps me to avoid injury. Here are a few tricks I've learned which help relieve the monotony of circling the track:

1. Don't count the laps; this can drive you crazy. To determine the distance you run, wear a watch and time one lap, determine your speed, then simply measure your final distance by noting the total time you have been out. For example, I usually run for two hours on the track. I time one lap and find that it is 2:05. I round this off to two minutes. That is simply an eight-minute mile, and eight divided into 120 minutes (two hours) gives 15 miles for the total run.

2. Don't run on the inside lane. Run in the middle of the track, in about the third or fourth lane. The track surface is usually superior here. Running a few inches from the concrete curb of a track requires that you constantly be alert to the possibility of hitting it with the foot. By moving to the center of the track, the mind is freed to think of more pleasant things.

3. Now and then, alternate direction. When I do long track workouts, I turn around every half-hour. This can be surprisingly refreshing.

4. Concentrate on anything interesting, except circling the track. Only on the track can the runner be free of the

need to look out for cars, dogs, and stones and holes. Here he can pretend that he is sitting at home in a chair thinking of whatever he pleases.

5. Intersperse other exercises throughout the run. For example, I might stop every quarter-hour and do 10 pushups. Now and then, I stop and walk one lap briskly. It is fun to see how fast you can walk.

6. Wear a sun visor. Not only will this protect the eyes and skin from excessive exposure (particularly at sunrise and sunset), but it can help you forget that you are on a track. Pull the visor down low so that you can't see more than 5-10 yards down the track. Now, you can go anywhere you want in the world of imagination. You can't see the stadium, so you can pretend you are anywhere. I find this to be a most enjoyable mental trick, and once again you can only do this safely on a track.

7. Tracks can be especially beautiful at night. Frequently, I'll stop, do my 10 pushups, then roll over on my back and stare at the sky. In the silence of the night, the heavens spread from horizon to horizon give an uplifting vista. I've even brought a star chart with me, and learned the constellations and planets in this way.

8. Finally, when all else fails, I think of George Littlewood who was a famous walker and runner about 100 years ago. Littlewood set a record by covering 623¾ miles in six days on a track measuring eight laps to the mile indoors at Madison Square Garden in 1888. When I tire of many laps, I recall that he once gave an exhibition on a circus ring measuring 38 laps to the mile by circling it for a total of 378 miles!

74. Is it good to train with other runners?

Pleasant conversation can make the miles pass by more quickly when taking a long, slow run. But be sure to pick training partners who won't accelerate the pace. I hate to be out 10 miles from home and continually find myself entreating my partner to slow down.

I feel that it's best to do sharpening workouts alone. It is almost impossible to do speed runs without racing your companions. What's more, I can't concentrate on relaxing when I'm also watching someone else.

However, I like to have a training partner for time-trials. Here, I can better simulate actual race conditions. If my partner is much better than I, then we sometimes make it a handicap, or I might run the last two miles of his four-mile time-trial.

75. How can I estimate the distance I've run?

The simplest method, as mentioned earlier, is to time the workout, then estimate the pace and compute the distance. For example, I might run for one hour at a pace that I estimate to be eight minutes per mile. Eight divided into 60 minutes gives 7½ miles for the workout.

The great advantage of this method over all others is that it frees the runner to modify the training course at any time. I frequently leave home wanting to cover, say, 15

A close finish in the Atlantic City Marathon in 1974. Left to right: Hugh Sweeny, 2:34:22; Tom Osler, 2:34:24; and Larry Connolly, 2:34:30. (Photo by Gregg Kohl, Atlantic City Press)

miles without any particular course in mind. I will simply wander here and there until two hours elapse, and the workout is then complete (assuming that my pace is eight minutes per mile).

If you want very accurate measurements of your training courses, you should purchase U.S. Geological Survey maps which cover your area. At a good stationery store you can purchase a small device which is designed to measure distance from these maps. It's nothing more than a miniature measuring wheel.

The Philadelphia Marathon course in Fairmount Park was first measured in this simple way. When the course was finally measured for certification using the difficult calibrated bicycle method, we found that the original measurement was only 64 yards too long in 26.2 miles!

76. Can I train right after eating?

This is an individual matter. In most cases, it is best to wait two or more hours after eating before running. I find that I need up to four hours abstinence before running a fast time-trial but only about one hour before a long, slow run.

On occasion, I am forced to train right after a large meal. In this case, I begin by alternately walking and running slow quarter-miles. After I cover 2-3 miles, I usually feel well enough to run continuously. I don't make a habit of doing this, however.

77. Should I train in the rain?

Only during very hot weather. All nature seeks shelter in the rain. Only runners insist on training in all kinds of weather. I had so many minor injuries and colds precipitated from training in cold damp weather that I finally decided never to train during a cold rain again. I have never regretted this decision. There are so few days when it rains here on the East Coast that I lose very little conditioning by not running on them.

78. What is the best time of the day for training?

Nearly everyone feels better running in the early afternoon than they do in the morning. Try running a time-trial at two miles at 8 a.m. and then next week try it at 3 p.m. All other things being equal, you will probably run 20-30 seconds faster in the afternoon. The body seems to need all that time to get "warmed up" for hard physical activity.

However, most runners have no choice in the time at which training can occur. Job and family considerations must come first. Slow running can be done at any hour of the day or night. Fast running, however, should be avoided in the very early morning hours. It is easier to damage tendons when they are not yet loosened up. If you must do speed work in the morning, then take a very long and thorough warmup.

79. Is it better to train once or twice daily?

This is a controversial question. I'm not sure myself. Ted Corbitt, one of the most experienced runners who ever set foot on the track, claims that only the total daily mileage matters. He claims that running one 20-mile run has the same training effect as running two 10-mile runs, one in the morning and one in the afternoon.

Arthur Lydiard disagrees. He feels that it is best to do one 20-miler. I'm not sure, but I lean toward Lydiard on this point.

80. Is it wise to train hard twice a day?

Definitely not! You can't recover from a hard workout in less than 24 hours. If you run fast in one workout, then you must run easily and slowly in the other in order to avoid the dangers of overstress.

81. How much sleep does a distance runner need?

I don't believe that distance runners require any more or less sleep than non-runners. Each individual has his own ideal sleeping pattern and quantity. I only sleep about five hours each night, usually rising at 3 or 4 a.m., at which time I often go out and run. I always have a 1-2-hour nap in the afternoon, however. Thus, I get a total of about 6-7 hours of sleep each day.

When I go into very hard training, I often find that I

desire an additional hour's sleep. I don't worry about this. However, when I find myself sleeping 10 or 11 hours per day, then I know that I'm very rundown and must reduce my training.

Oddly, under extreme fatigue, it is difficult to sleep at all. For example, following an all-out marathon race, I frequently find it difficult to fall asleep. The body is so active trying to rebuild itself from the damage done in racing that I simply can't slow the system down enough for sleep. You certainly should not endure this kind of strain frequently.

82. Is there anything I can do to assist my body in recovering from a day's workout?

Yes, there are a few acts that hasten recovery:

1. If you can, take a one-hour nap about two hours after running. (Unfortunately, most of us can't afford this luxury.)

2. Avoid standing and slow walking. This makes it difficult for the heart to pump the blood from the lower legs. Retarding the circulation means that the waste products of fatigue are remaining in the legs.

3. Brisk walking for up to one hour helps to restore the legs to their recovered state. Brisk walking promotes vigorous circulation and hastens the removal of fatigue products. It also provides a gentle and safe form of stretching for the legs.

83. Is there an ideal running style?

No. As Emil Zatopek once said, "They do not award medals for picturesque form." Each runner has a different bone structure and different strength ratios within his muscular system. Therefore, the form that is best for you might be poor for me. Nevertheless, there are a few aspects of proper running form that are universal:

1. Don't reach out and try artificially to lengthen your stride. Without thinking about it, you should adjust the stride to the length that is most efficient for the given

speed. In general, a short stride is more efficient than a long one.

2. Don't throw your head back. The angle of the head sets the angle of all other components of the body. Simply look down at the track at a distance of about 10-20 yards from your feet. Everything else will automatically fall into place.

3. When the foot first makes contact with the ground, it should be with the heel, and not the ball of the foot. The best way to determine how you land is to examine the soles of your shoes. If the heel area is wearing most rapidly, then you are landing properly. If the area near the ball of the foot is wearing out first (especially behind the little toe), then you are landing too far forward. By landing on the ball of the foot, the shock of ground contact is absorbed in the calf muscles. This is tiring in very long runs, but tolerable in sprints and middle-distance races under one mile. By landing on the heel, the calf is rested and the shock is absorbed in the bones.

84. Is there an exercise I can perform which will improve the efficiency of my running form?

Yes. When I was in high school, Dr. William Ruthrauff, an expert in figure skating, taught me a simple exercise to perform while running which I have used on and off for the past 20 years with remarkable success.

Ruthrauff was not a runner himself, but he did make a careful study of running form. He had a theory that there were two types of running action which he called "trotting" and "pacing" after the terms used in horse racing. I could never understand the mechanical principles he was trying to teach me, but the exercise is easy to learn.

Simply grasp the elastic band of your running shorts with your thumbs. In a relaxed fashion, hold onto your trunks (as if they might fall off) and continue running without further concern. Automatically, the motion of the arms will adjust itself to the artificial harness thus created. After about one week of running this way, let go of the trunks and you should feel that you are a bit closer to the ground and there is less wasted motion in your upper body.

Ted Corbitt and Jack Barry were two of America's greatest runners in their day, and they also were students of Ruthrauff. I consider myself fortunate to have known him in the final years of his life.

85. How should I warm up before training?

This depends on the time of day and the type of workout you anticipate. Early in the morning, I always begin by walking mixed with running for one mile. The walking segments should be brisk and about 50 yards in length. In the afternoon, I can frequently begin with very slow running and then just gradually increase the speed until the desired training pace is reached.

When doing long, slow workouts, no more than one mile of slow running or walking and running should be necessary. Before speed workouts, however, much more work should be done. I find it necessary to run for at least 20-30 minutes at a slow pace before attempting any fast running. When I was a teenager, I only needed a two-minute jog, but now I require more than 10 times that amount. Also, try several short sprints before a time-trial or race. It is wise to allow the legs to undergo the full range of motion *before* the serious trial begins.

86. How should I cool down after training?

After most workouts, a short walk of about 100 yards is all that is needed. In particular don't sit down immediately, but keep moving. Your body will tell you to do this.

After very hard workouts, it is a good idea to take a serious cooldown in order to promote the removal of waste products. This should include two or three miles of the slowest running followed by another mile or two of brisk walking mixed with short runs.

After a really hard effort, such as an all-out marathon race, the runner should try to keep his circulation going vigorously for some time. Three miles of brisk walking would be an excellent start on the road to recovery. The worst thing you can do is stop immediately upon crossing the finish line and stand around talking to friends. Remember, standing retards circulation in the lower legs.

Also, be sure to stay warm during this cooldown period. It would be very easy to catch a cold when your resistance is at its lowest.

87. Does a runner's personality change as he grows weary during a workout?

As fatigue develops, runners become irritable and very aggressive. I have watched people who are normally shy and retiring become transformed into daring fighters in the final stages of a run. This is dangerous, because under fatigue the runner is likely to do things that he will regret later. For example, runners will defy traffic as though the cars would bounce right off them were they hit.

By being aware that your personality becomes altered in this way, you can take precautions against it. When I see a confrontation about to develop between me and someone else after I've run many miles, I always stop myself from following my impulses and try to leave the scene as quickly and gracefully as the situation permits. When I stay there, I usually get myself into trouble that I find embarrassing later.

88. What situations arise that require a runner to "keep his cool"?

Any longtime runner has interesting stories to tell about his adventures on the road. In 1964, I was out in the snow running 15 miles. It was a bitter day, and before the present era in which runners are an accepted part of the landscape. To make matters worse, I was wearing ordinary street clothing. Even my shoes did not identify me as an athlete in training.

As I ran down the left side of the park road, I noticed a police car coming toward me on the shoulder of the road. I motioned to the officer to leave me room, but he continued coming right for me. He stopped about 10 yards in front of me. I thought this was unusual but was used to harassment on the road.

As I went past the door of his car, calmly minding my own business, the policeman popped out like a jack-in-the-box and tackled me. Before I knew what was happening, I was in the car beside him. I was furious, thinking that he was harassing me for running.

He called in over his radio and said, "I've got him."

I looked at him and replied, "You've got yourself one heap of trouble, that's what you've got!"

He seemed quite startled by my self-assurance and description of how I would have him run off the police force. As I mentioned, fatigue changes your personality and makes you very aggressive. For some reason, he believed my story and let me run back home.

Later, I learned that he was only doing his sworn duty. It seems that a stolen car full of teenagers had been ditched in the park, and the culprits had run off in all directions. Since almost no one ran for fun or health in those days, it was only reasonable that I should have been identified as one of the thieves. From that day on, I dressed like a runner.

Another interesting incident is told by my friend Ted Corbitt. Corbitt is a New Yorker and America's most famous ultra-marathoner. He works as a physical therapist in downtown Manhattan, and frequently runs to and from work on the city streets.

One day, he was charged by a German police dog which was owned by a cripple holding a crutch. Ted reached for a stone and threw it at the dog but missed. At this, the owner shouted that he would break his crutches over Ted's head. As the dog continued to menace him, Ted could picture a headline in the afternoon *Daily News:* "Physical Therapist Slugs Crippled Man." A reminder that having his dog off his leash was illegal did no good, and Ted made a quick exit before his worst fears became reality.

89. What about the runner's constant enemy, the dog?

Dogs are really more of a nuisance than a serious threat. Yet most runners I know fear dogs more than they do motor vehicles. I've never heard of a runner being killed or maimed by a dog, but I know of several who lost their battle with the automobile.

90. Can I run away from an attacking dog?

No, indeed! The dog is even faster than a horse. By running away from the animal, you increase your chances of being bitten tenfold.

91. What should I do if a dog threatens to attack?

There are two general methods for handling this situation. The first is based on making peace with the dog; the second requires that you stare him down and convince him that you are dominant. I like the second method.

If a dog comes running at you, barking and threatening, first stop and face the dog. In most cases, he too will stop. You can then begin to walk away from the dog, while still facing him, until you are out of his range. Then, cautiously begin running again.

At times, the dog will continue to run at you after you have stopped. In this case shout at him loudly: "Halt!" or "Stop!" or "Get back!" Raise your arms and threaten him. Grab a stick and shake it at him. I've never seen a dog continue after such a display.

Never turn your back on the dog until you are thoroughly convinced that he has retreated for good. Remember, most dog bites occur from the rear. I have twice been bitten by dogs. In both cases, I did not even see the dog until he had nipped me.

The procedure outlined here is very effective. It is important not to fear the dog. Somehow, they seem to know when you fear them, and then it's twice as hard to stare them down.

92. Do thin runners respond to training differently than heavy runners?

Yes, they do. Runners who are naturally lean, and fail to gain weight even when not training, usually require less work. They can often race quite well on half the training required by their counterparts who are heavily muscled and who gain weight at the mere sight of food. Not only do they require less work; they are also frail and would likely break down under heavy training.

Muscular runners can take more abuse in training without injury. It is interesting to note that there is a higher percentage of "big men" in ultra-marathoning than in marathoning. Greater muscle mass may be needed here to absorb the abuse of so many miles. Also, a good strong stomach is needed to supply the energy needs that must be replaced during the race itself.

93. List negative obsessions that runners develop on racing and training.

Some runners make a fetish out of never missing a day's training. Their streaks of continuous days running can number into the years. There is probably no direct harm in this. However, it distracts the runner from his legitimate concerns. He should first concentrate on listening to his body. Take a day off if the body needs it. There is no loss but actually a gain in such actions.

Another obsession runners succumb to is the minimum-mileage-for-the-week syndrome. Runners will kill themselves to make that magic 60 miles or 100 miles, or whatever it may be. Again, this distracts the runner from his first concern. He should be monitoring his training according to how he feels and not according to some preassigned silly number.

A dangerous obsession is the refusal to quit in races. Of course, there is no honor quitting simply because you are being beaten. There are, however, times when continuing poses a real threat to your health. At such times, it is the wise runner who quits.

PART TWO
Staying Healthy

6
INJURIES
AND ILLNESSES

94. Is injury common among distance runners?

It certainly is! Go to any race and canvas the runners. You will find that half of them are at that moment troubled by sore tendons in some part of the foot or leg. Perhaps the injury is not yet sufficiently serious to terminate their ability to race, but it inhibits their enjoyment of running and their performance in racing. Almost every runner in the race will tell you that within the past few years he suffered an injury that became so serious he virtually was forced to stop running.

95. What injuries are common to runners?

Inflammation of the tendons in the heel, knee and hip is probably the most frequent problem. Fortunately, it is in most cases not serious enough to completely terminate training and racing. Less often, runners suffer actual muscle pulls or tears. These happen in the thigh or calf.

Other trouble seems to originate in certain misalignments of the bones. These can cause pressure on a nerve that can send shooting pain into an area of the leg or the entire leg. The pain is every bit as bad as when there is actual tendon or muscle irritation.

96. In most cases, could these injuries have been prevented?

In 99% of the cases, yes. Nearly all running injuries are the result of overtaxing the body. As the runner grows weary, his steps become less certain. He is more likely to step on a stone or to twist his leg in some unexpected rut. In addition, a tired body is not able to heal itself effectively. Once injury begins, it can grow steadily worse when the runner lacks the vital energy reserves that are necessary for a self-cure.

Because some level of fatigue is always present in endurance activities, *injury becomes the runner's shadow.* It stalks him with every step. The farther and faster he runs, the more likely that injury will strike.

97. How, then, can these injuries be prevented?

By staying fresh and feeling good. Only on very exceptional days should the runner allow himself to grow so tired that injury becomes likely. When a runner is training properly, he should look and feel good, and be productive in his everyday affairs. When he feels tired and washed out, he needs rest and not stress.

By maintaining a high level of general vitality, the runner will be less likely to encounter minor accidents such as stepping in a hole. When minor problems do occur, his body will be sufficiently vigorous to initiate self-repair.

98. Can you describe specific symptoms of overwork that point toward potential injury?

There are several symptoms of overstress which every runner must learn to detect. Here are the key ones:

1. Mild leg soreness.

2. Lowered general resistance (evidenced by sniffles, headache, fever blisters, etc.).

3. Washed-out feeling and I-don't-care attitude.

4. Poor coordination (evidenced by general clumsiness, tripping, stubbing one's feet, poor auto driving, etc.).

5. Hangover from previous run.

Notice that these symptoms are very mild. They are not dramatic. The runner must become aware of his body's fine tuning. This is not easy, but a high level of self-awareness is necessary to avoid the aggravation of injury. Most runners ignore these very mild symptoms, thinking that they are trivial. They are the only warning he will get in most cases.

99. Why is it so difficult for runners to detect these symptoms of overstress?

All good distance racers learn to minimize the feeling of discomfort that can be quite heavy in the final stages of a race. Runners even make a mystique about enduring suffering. In many cases, great respect is awarded the athlete who appears to have triumphed over pain by driving himself on when others would have stopped. There is no doubt that such heroics can win races!

But you can't endure this form of self-abuse too often, or your career as a runner will be remarkably short. Nature will stop you by making you a cripple if you lack the common sense necessary to protect your health.

Rather than learning to ignore discomfort, the runner must learn to detect even its most minute traces. Once detected, he must know what action is called for. In training, one must learn to stop at the halfway point. In other words, the training session should end at the point where the runner could turn around and repeat the entire workout.

In racing, a much greater degree of fatigue must be endured for success. For this reason, a runner must learn not to race "all-out" except on the most important occasions. He must learn how to race with a measured effort.

100. Summarize the key to injury prevention.

It is a simple commonsense principle. When we feel good, look good, and are alert and productive, our bodies are adapting effectively to stresses (like running) which we place upon them. If we feel tired, pain and washed out, we need rest, not stress.

101. Frankly, I'm skeptical. Can it really be that simple? I suppose you don't ever get injured anymore.

The principle is simple, but its application requires a great deal of self-control. It is not easy to reduce training mileage when unexpected symptoms of fatigue arise. We want so badly to be in top condition for the coming race. It's especially hard to stay away from a big race that you worked toward for months. How difficult it is to explain to your running friends that you won't be going with them to the big marathon. Ah, pride . . . a deadly sin!

My own medical case history is interesting in this regard. I began running in 1954, and for the first 10 years I foolishly overworked myself, thinking I was made of iron rather than mere flesh. As a result, I developed a particularly bad case of achilles tendinitis while in high school and runner's knee while in college.

Finally, I had a sciatic nerve condition in 1964 that left me almost unable to walk. I still remember going out to train and going so slowly due to hip pain that even the dogs looked at me puzzled. They couldn't decide if I was running or not and were confused as to whether to chase me.

After an osteopath relocated my hip, I took a long, deep, soul-searching study of my training diary. It was here that I finally realized that fatigue was the culprit and formulated the list of dangerous symptoms I've mentioned earlier. From that point on, I was trouble-free for eight straight years. From the ages of 24 through 32, I did my hardest racing and training without the slightest injury. I felt invincible!

I had boasted to Dr. George Sheehan of my eight injury-free years, and he suggested that I write up my thoughts on prevention for his forthcoming *Encyclopedia of Athletic Medicine*. It was April 1972, and that month means the Boston Marathon. Unfortunately, I came down with a bad stomach virus which gave me both fever and vomiting. As I lay in bed, I wrote the article on prevention. Somehow, putting this concept into words for other runners made me foolishly feel that I was above it. After all, I had not been hurt in eight years.

Three days after rising from bed, my legs felt completely dead, yet I packed my bags for Boston. I was doing the very thing that I had just written against. How dangerous this sport is when we feel that we are bigger than nature! I ran one of my worst marathons, really dying in the final miles. For two months thereafter, I could hardly move in my workouts. Finally, in July, I dislocated a cuboid bone in my foot. For nine months, I ran in pain on this foot until Jack Brickley, a runner and surgeon-podiatrist managed to effect a cure.

Two years later, I again had sciatic trouble which kept me off the road for one month. This, I believe, was due to stretching exercises which I now oppose and will speak of shortly.

Heavy mileage can be dangerous, because you start to get careless as you grow weary. In July 1976, I was attempting to break my record for one week's running—216 miles. I had 198 miles in for the week, and had run 20 miles early in the morning. It was quite hot and humid when I left for my afternoon run. I selected a path in the dark shade of several large trees on the campus.

In my weariness and the darkness caused by the shade trees, I missed seeing a sharp broken bottle which placed a deep two-inch cut in my ankle. I was unable to run for one month after this injury, and felt pain there, on and off, for about six months.

My score is now three injuries in the past 13 years!

102. I have heard that stretching exercises help to prevent injury. Is this true?

I must warn my reader that I am about to commit heresy. Every coach and doctor I know of today advocates stretching exercises as the way to prevent injury in runners. I emphatically disagree.

Those who advocate stretching reason as follows: Long-distance running tends to decrease the athlete's general flexibility. The muscles and tendons grow tight. There is a decrease in the range of movement in the leg. Few runners can touch their toes with the knees held straight. With the tendons and muscles under greater than normal tension, injury is more likely. By doing stretching exercises, this undesirable tightening is reversed, the range of movement increases, and the runner regains his lost suppleness.

It sounds great in theory, but in practice it doesn't appear (at least to me) to work. Runners tend to be tired. Their muscles and tendons are in a state of mild irritability from all this unnatural work. By stretching them, they add even more irritation. Sooner or later, the strain of stretching itself induces injury. I believe my last injury, a sciatic nerve condition in 1974, was precipitated in this way. From 1964-72, when I raced without injury, I never once stretched. In those days, the prophets of stretching had not emerged. I bought the idea in 1973, and became injured in '74 as a result. Never again! Many of my running companions have had similar experiences.

Since my avoidance of stretching exercises is very unorthodox, you are likely to discard my experience and conclude that I am a singular case who has been very lucky in avoiding injury. Nevertheless, if you decide to perform stretching exercises, approach them with the greatest caution. If pain appears in some tendons while running, immediately suspect the stretching itself as a possible cause. Curtailing these exercises for a few weeks might result in reversal of the injury.

103. How does sleep relate to injury and its prevention?

An athlete in heavy training should be able to sleep as long as he wants. However, the runner who needs more than nine hours sleep per night is probably overtraining. In general, runners require no more sleep than those who do not train.

A very important consideration is the sleeping surface. This should be flat and very firm. A soft mattress can lead to back strain which in turn can result in numerous leg problems. I once had severe pain in one knee and found that it disappeared quickly after I began sleeping on the floor.

104. When an injury does occur, should I stop running?

In nearly all cases, racing should be terminated, but mild running and walking should continue. Most running injuries heal far faster if the runner can stay on his feet with gentle activity than if the runner stops training completely.

Frequently, I have seen runners cease training for several months due to injury. When they start training again, they frequently rediscover the injury in the very same state as when they stopped running months ago. The body seems to neglect repairing itself when we tell it that it no longer has to work. Mild short runs and walks increase the circulation to the injury, and remind the body that there is work to be done and that healing is required.

105. What kind of training should I do when I'm injured?

First, there must absolutely be no fast running. All racing should cease. The pain generated by the injury should be used to monitor the training. If the injury hurts at the beginning of training but gradually disappears after a mile or two, then long, slow running is probably safe. Be sure, however, that the injury does not grow worse on successive days. Use common sense.

If the pain of the injury does not lessen after running a few miles, then try brisk walking mixed with running. If the pain is quite bad, perhaps only walking should be allowed. In extreme cases, swimming or bicycling can be used to stimulate the circulation while nature heals the injury.

If the runner has been doing stretching exercises, this is one time he should stop them entirely. It is not unlikely that the injury is due to the stretching itself. In any case, stretching will aggravate the injury and retard the recovery process.

106. Should I go to a doctor immediately upon being injured?

In the case of most doctors, no. The ordinary physician has little knowledge or experience with runners. He is trained in the diseases of the sickly. You are a very fit creature, and you require different treatment.

First, discuss your problem with several experienced runners. In most cases, your injury will be one common to the sport, and their advice is worth far more than the doctor's. If you must see a doctor, then find one who is himself a runner. In general, I would not trust anyone else to understand your particular situation.

107. How should I handle visits to the doctor?

Most doctors I've met treat their patients like little children. They expect you to accept their advice with little questioning. They are also far too quick to recommend medications that can be dangerous to the athlete who relies so much on the very fine tuning of his body.

When visiting the doctor, I would recommend the following:

1. If at all possible, he should come highly recommended by experienced runners. Better yet, he should be a runner himself.

2. First tell him that you are in his office *for diagnosis and discussion only.* You will consider the possibility of treatment *only after all alternatives are clear and you have had time to reflect on them.*

3. Allow the doctor to do harmless diagnostic tests such as a visual examination and X-rays.

4. After hearing the treatment he recommends, go home and discuss it with other runners. Be conservative. I would feel free to accept treatments in the form of whirlpool baths, manipulation and similar techniques. Shoe alterations and orthotics are also treatments that can do little damage.

5. Accept injections such as cortisone only after everything else has been tried and you are about to retire. These

are very dangerous, and many doctors act as though they are harmless. These injections reduce the pain, but the injury remains. Without feeling pain, many athletes have turned minor problems into crippling injuries.

6. Surgery is another desperate attempt at cure. Again, consider this only after everything else has failed and you cannot run. I have met many runners who have been under the knife, and several have regretted it.

7. Finally, remember that God heals and the doctor sends the bill. Give nature every chance to do her own good work.

108. What can be done for sore heels?

Perhaps the most common complaint of runners is achilles tendinitis. In many cases, this is due to strain being placed on the tendons in the heel. I injured my achilles tendons when 16 years old by doing sprints in running shoes with low heels. The low heels made the tendon stretch too far and caused very painful irritation. Like most injuries I've had, it never completely healed. When in mild training, the heels will be very quiet, but when I increase my mileage, they frequently remind me of their presence.

There is a simple remedy for this problem which works wonderfully in most cases. Simply elevate the heel. This can be done in one of two ways:

1. Glue an additional heel made of crepe rubber an eighth- to a quarter-inch thick to the bottom of the shoes. This is the preferable treatment.

2. Simply add sponge rubber heel pads to the inside of the shoes. Unfortunately, this simple technique might spoil the "fit" of the shoe.

Frequently, these remedies are so effective that the pain in the heel is noticeably reduced in the very first workout using these modified shoes.

109. How should I handle blisters, nail problems and the like?

With shoes that fit your feet properly, these will very rarely occur. I even run 50-mile races without socks and have no difficulty.

When I do get blisters, I open them myself and let them drain. I cut away all the dead skin, rub petroleum jelly into the tender red area, then cover it with gauze and a bandage.

Any podiatrist can do wonders with blisters and damaged nails. He does not need to have experience with runners to handle these problems. In most cases, the podiatrist can provide immediate relief to the extent that you can immediately resume running.

110. Do runners frequently catch colds?

Minor infections are an indication that the body is being overtaxed. They indicate that training and racing should be reduced in intensity. The runner who senses in his bones the appropriate level of work will find that he enjoys robust health and is rarely sick. Unfortunately, such runners are rare.

These days, we hear much about vitamin C as a cold-preventative. This is a folly that we modern Americans love. How sweet it would be to simply pop a few pills and then find that our problems vanish. Reality isn't that simple. Good health is, to a degree, earned. When one takes good care of his body and avoids abusing it, then it is likely to reward him by functioning in a state of robust vigor. You can't expect to race hard, train hard, sleep little and overeat, and to be free of colds simply by gulping vitamin C tablets.

111. If I catch a cold, should I stop training?

It depends on the severity of your illness. If you simply experience a running nose and sneezing, then mild running might actually help break the cold. If, however, you have a fever, then you had best go to bed rather than the track.

112. Should I take medication for minor infections like colds?

Definitely not! It is far better to go to bed and let nature heal you. All medications have serious side-effects. This

Osler (far left) begins the final lap of his 1976 24-hour run of 114 miles. (Photo by Ed Dodd)

means that after you recover from the illness, you must then recover from the treatment. When you let nature heal you, there are no side-effects. True, it may take a few days longer, but when you return to the road you will feel far better.

Many medications dispensed by doctors will very seriously retard a runner's racing performance for weeks after the symptoms of the disease have vanished. This might be fine for the inactive person, but it can be very discouraging to the competitive athlete.

Of course, there are extreme cases where one should seek medical help. However, it is generally wise to rest, eat well and relax rather than rush to the physician.

113. I've just recovered from illness and now feel ready to return to the road. How should I train?

Let us suppose you have suffered a minor virus infection and have rested for five days. You have a few sniffles left, but no cough or fever. You feel that your body has the problem under control. You are now ready to try the following training plan designed to return you to normal training in one week:

1. Divide the length of your medium runs by about seven, and slowly run this distance the first day. You might feel rather uncomfortable. Weakness, side stitch and leg soreness are often present.

2. On the second day, add one-seventh of your medium training to the first day's mileage. (For example, if you ran one mile yesterday, today you run two miles.) *You should observe that you feel much better than you did yesterday.* If you don't, you should return to rest, for you are not ready for running.

3. Each day, you add an additional one-seventh of your medium mileage to the previous day's run. Although you are running farther each day, you should be feeling better.

4. After seven days, you should feel ready for normal training.

The important key to this recovery plan is found in its gradual increase in mileage and the requirement that the runner feel better as the days progress. In no case should the runner attempt fast work until recovery is 100% complete.

114. How do allergies affect a runner's performance?

I suffer from a rather bad case of hay fever in the late summer and rose fever in the late spring. Both allergies weaken me, and I no longer race while they are in progress. I usually continue my normal workouts but avoid anything exceptionally hard. Any medications I tried made me very drowsy. This lifeless feeling seemed as bad as the irritation from the hay fever. Consequently, I now avoid all medications and simply live with it.

Allergies are not to be taken lightly. They place a severe strain on the body. Three times during my running career, I have urinated blood. This is a sign of the greatest strain. All three incidents occurred after running very hard during my allergy season. This is why I no longer race at this time.

It is interesting to note that my diet affects the degree to which I suffer. By avoiding rich foods, such as cake, pie, ice cream and all products containing sugar or honey, my allergy symptoms are reduced considerably.

115. Can running cause hemorrhoids?

Yes, indirectly it can. In 1963, I was taking an easy 18-mile workout in preparation for the Atlantic City Marathon. With four miles remaining, I felt the need for a bowel movement. But I was interested in timing this workout and did not want to stop. Besides, the pressure was quite mild.

The next day, I realized the folly of not stopping when I developed a hemorrhoid about the size of a peanut. The Atlantic City Marathon was only three weeks away, and I was very concerned that I would be unable to compete. A physician recommended that I use cortisone suppositories in addition to frequently squatting in a tub of water that was as hot as I could tolerate.

In two weeks, the hemorrhoid disappeared and I ran my first marathon under three hours, 2:41:59 at Atlantic City.

Should I feel the need for a bowel movement while running, I always stop for relief before continuing. In this way, I have avoided further hemorrhoids.

116. What is the most unusual recovery from an injury that you have experienced?

Without doubt, my most remarkable recovery occurred in 1974 when I was suffering from my second attack of a sciatic nerve problem. I was running a one-hour track race on a hot, humid night in July. At about six miles, I felt a shooting pain blaze from my left hip down to my foot. I immediately reduced my pace and the pain left.

In my final two miles, the leader lapped me and asked me to stay with him. As I accelerated, the pain returned. It was sharp and did not disappear when I again slowed down. I should have stopped right on the spot, but instead I foolishly limped lap after lap to salvage second place.

Several days later, when the pain failed to diminish, I

visited a good chiropractor who is also a runner. He was unable to give me any relief. For one month, I tried running at 10-12 minutes per mile, but the sharp pain still persisted.

A young professor with whom I had been working that summer was suddenly stricken with a brain hemorrhage and died. He lived only a few blocks from me and had a young family similar to my own. I attended funeral services at the local Lutheran church. As I sat there, I saw his widow and children enter. It was all too easy for me to identify with the grief, since I could picture my own wife and children facing similar tragedy. Deep emotion swelled within me, and I felt waves of heat and cold rushing through my body. It was all I could do to restrain the ocean of tears that seemed to engulf me.

When I arrived home from the service, I reached down to untie my shoes. This simple act had resulted in sharp pain every time it was executed since the injury, and I automatically flinched in anticipation of the pain. Surprisingly, there was none. Could it be that I was cured?

That night, I went out and ran seven miles at a brisk pace. It was my first night of painless running in more than a month. The next day, I ran 10 miles and the next 17. The pain never returned.

What happened? Some healings defy explanation.

7
CHOOSING AND CHANGING SHOES

117. Is there an ideal running shoe?

No, shoes are a highly individual matter. The shape of the runner's foot must match the last around which the shoe was constructed. Runners vary in their need for heel lift, heel width, sole bend, shank support, heel counter and other features.

118. What features are essential in a good running shoe?

1. The sole must be made of a material that will soften the shock of landing. Many shoes have a sole constructed of hard rubber so that it will be durable. Unfortunately, hard rubber does not have sufficient "give" to absorb shock. In this case, the shoe survives, while the runner breaks down. Remember, good running shoes cannot have a durable sole.

2. The sole should bend where your foot can bend. Too many running shoes are stiff under the ball of the foot. This makes it awkward to drive powerfully off the toes.

3. The uppers should be soft and supple. In most cases, socks should not be necessary even for the longest runs. Unless you are running in snow, nylon is a better material for the upper than leather.

4. The shoe should be free of needless trimmings. Many nylon shoes have various areas of "reinforcement," usually made of suede leather. These are usually useless, and I frequently cut them off before running in the shoe.

119. Do worn shoes contribute to injury?

Yes, worn shoes are a frequent source of injury. The shoe is not static but dynamic. Each time you run in it, it becomes altered slightly. After one week of hard training, it can change enough to have altered the runner's stride significantly without his realizing it. The most common problem occurs at the heel where the shoes usually wear on the outer edge of the sole. Figure One illustrates the typical wear pattern. These heels must be rebuilt quickly, or leg injury is likely to occur.

Fig. 1. Unworn and worn heels compared.

In some cases, the sole wears excessively under the ball of the foot. This condition is more difficult to repair successfully and usually requires that new shoes be obtained.

120. Should runners learn to make simple modifications of their shoes?

Yes, because these can greatly increase comfort and significantly reduce the chance of injury. I do not know of any running shoe that I can wear straight from the dealer without first making some modification. I usually have to make more room in the toe area by making a slit across the front of the shoe. I remove all unnecessary trim, which not only reduces the shoe's weight, but also makes it more comfortable. I usually increase the heel lift and sometimes glue an additional slab of soft rubber to the bottom of the sole.

121. What tools are required for shoe modification?

Only the simplest tools, available at any hardware store, are needed. Figure Two illustrates these. Required:

1. A utility knife with extra blades. This must be razor sharp, as it is used to cut rubber, nylon and leather.

2. A hand file. This is used to roughen materials before gluing.

3. A hacksaw, for adjusting the shape of the rubber sole.

4. Contact cement, for gluing additional rubber to the sole.

122. Where can I purchase rubber for modifying the sole?

For the simplest modifications, no purchase is required. One can use pieces of rubber from the soles of discarded shoes and rubber from an old tire tube (especially a truck tire tube).

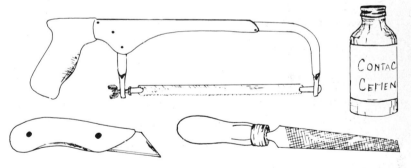

Fig. 2. The simple tools needed for shoe modification.

For more extensive repairs, it is best to purchase large rectangles of new rubber. Locate the supplier of shoe repair shops in your area by the phone directory or by inquiry at a repair shop. The supplier will require that you purchase wholesale, but this is no trouble as the materials are inexpensive.

Ask him to let you browse through his warehouse. Examine the various grades and thicknesses of rubber available. I buy the softest crepe rubber I can find. This usually costs about six dollars for a sheet 2×3 feet. He can also sell you a contact cement that is designed for use with the rubber. Barge Cement is fine.

123. This sounds like it's going to be troublesome. Why not have a professional repairman do the job?

It won't be as hard as it seems. And professional repairmen often can't appreciate your needs and frequently do an unsatisfactory job. The few tricks necessary for shoe modification should be mastered by the serious runner so that he can experiment at his leisure and gradually learn to perfect his shoes to meet his own specific needs.

124. My toes feel cramped. What can I do?

I find it very difficult to locate a satisfactory running shoe that gives enough toe room. The front of a shoe should be boxy in shape so that the toes have room to spread as though they were clawing the ground while driving the body forward. Also, many runners lose toenails because of friction.

To remedy this situation, first cut off any leather reinforcement in the toe area. This might be all that is required. If not, then make a horizontal slit from left to right just a fraction of an inch above the sole. Don't be afraid to cut your nice new shoes. It's cheaper to do surgery on them than it is on your feet. Figure Three illustrates this cut.

Fig. 3. More room for the toes by making a slit.

Don't make this slit any wider than necessary. First, try one inch, then slowly widen it if needed. Once the front of the shoe is open, sand and small stones will on occasion work their way in while you are running.

125. My shoe is too high near the back of the ankle. What can I do?

Figure Four shows the problem area found on the back of many shoes today. This added material not only serves no purpose; it can frequently press into the Achilles tendon and cause it to become irritated.

Fig. 4. Some shoes have a tab on the rear that can be irritating to the tendons.

Here, the remedy is simple and obvious: cut it off. Don't worry that the shoe will fall apart. I have never seen this happen.

126. How can I keep the sole from wearing rapidly?

Good running shoes have soft rubber soles. They wear rapidly. This distortion of the sole must be prevented so that the legs do not become injured. Fortunately, there is a simple method that not only prevents injury but greatly increases the lifespan of the shoe:

1. Look at the bottoms of your old shoes and determine the area which wears fastest. Usually, this will be the heel.

2. When the shoes are new, glue a piece of tire tube over the area that gets the most wear. (See Figure Nine.)

3. Every few days, examine this patch to make sure it has not worn through. Once it is worn, tear it off and put a new one on. In this way, the sole will last almost indefinitely. I can obtain 1500 miles from a pair of shoes in this way.

127. Can't I use a glue-gun or spread on rubber from a tube for this purpose?

You can try, but the results are often unsatisfactory. When a patch of rubber is glued to the heel, it is uniform in thickness. The material from the glue-gun is not.

128. Exactly how is rubber glued to the sole of the shoe?

Care must be exercised when gluing the surfaces together so that the materials will not separate and the shoe fall apart while running.

1. Both contact surfaces must be clean and rough. Take a file and work on the shoe until a clean surface of new rubber emerges in the area where the gluing will occur.

2. Spread a thin coat of contact cement on both contact surfaces. If the weather is not very cold, it is best to do this outside. There are dangerous vapors from this glue which you must avoid breathing. Now wait 10-15 minutes while the glue dries. (Read the directions on the glue container for the exact time that it must set.)

3. Very carefully place the two surfaces together. Once they touch, you cannot move them apart; you don't get a second chance. Now, squeeze them together tightly. Since it is difficult to align the two pieces of rubber exactly, one piece should be too large so that it can be trimmed after the gluing is complete.

4. Contact cement does not require drying time. You can now take a utility knife and trim off the excess rubber. The shoe can now be used for running at once.

129. Demonstrate the various modifications you make to your own shoes.

Figure Five shows the shoe I prefer for my own racing and training needs, the Tiger Pinto. I'm not advocating this shoe for you; it just happens to be a good shell for my particular needs. I say "shell," because the shoe is too thin-soled for long running and requires considerable modification.

1. I remove the leather reinforcement in the toe area to allow my toes to spread. See Figure Six.

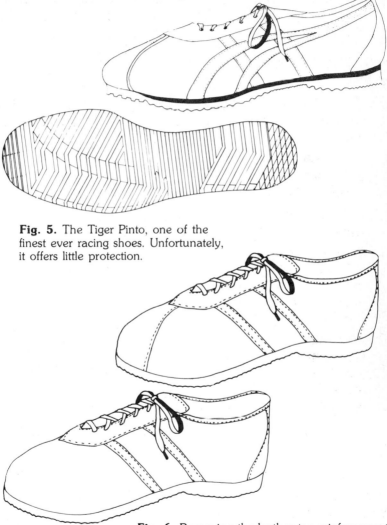

Fig. 5. The Tiger Pinto, one of the finest ever racing shoes. Unfortunately, it offers little protection.

Fig. 6. Removing the leather toe reinforcement.

2. I remove the stitching which holds the tongue. I do this because the tongue in its original position will cause the tops of my toes to chafe. The tongue is held in place now by using the shoe laces as shown in Figure Seven.

3. The heel on the Pinto is too low for my needs. Unless

I elevate it, my Achilles tendons will rebel and grow sore in just one workout. Figure Eight shows a quarter-inch slab of rubber added to the heel.

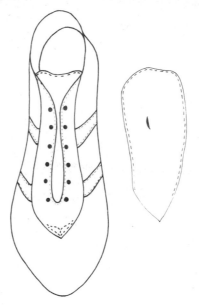

Fig. 7. Removing the tongue.

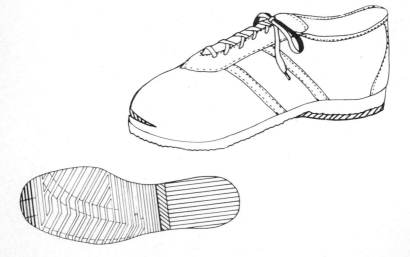

Fig. 8. An additional ¼-inch heel.

4. On my shoes, as on most runners' shoes, the heel area wears very quickly. In Figure Nine, I have glued an additional patch made of hard rubber from a discarded tire tube to the area which wears most rapidly. This shoe is now ready for light training and racing.

Fig. 9. The heel area protected by a tire tube patch. One of the simplest ways to extend shoe life.

5. For heavy training and very long races, I like to have additional soft rubber on the sole to absorb the shock of landing. In Figure 10, I show the same shoe as seen in Figure Eight with an additional piece of soft rubber on the sole. This can be from an eighth- to a quarter-inch thick. If the front of the shoe now feels too inflexible, horizontal slits can be made across the bottom of the sole under the ball of the foot.

Fig. 10. The entire sole covered by additional rubber to create a soft training shoe.

8
EATING AND DRINKING

130. Does the runner require a special diet?

No. The nutritional needs of the runner do not vary significantly from those of the non-athlete. This does not mean, however, that he should eat the great variety of prepared foods that are available in the supermarket.

The average American probably partakes of far too many fast convenience foods such as TV dinners and instant breakfasts. The runner, as well as the non-runner, should avoid these commercially-prepared products. He should, whenever possible, select his foods fresh, as they arrive from nature, and eat them with as little preparation as is necessary.

131. Are vitamin and mineral supplements necessary?

No. Many coaches have argued that high-potency supplements are required for the athlete in heavy training. My own experience does not reveal any such need. Frankly, I have little faith in man-made nutritional products.

The human body has evolved over millions of years. It was designed to obtain its nutrition from the great variety of natural foods found in the environment. Today, a Ph.D. with his degree in nutrition claims to know more than nature herself and can package our needs in a tiny capsule.

Wouldn't it be great if we could simply take a vitamin pill and then go eat all the junk food so readily available without fear of nutritional disaster? Life is not so simple, although most of us fall easy victims to this type of fraud.

Eat a great variety of wholesome fresh foods. Throw away the vitamin capsules.

132. What gives you the authority to dismiss the experts in nutrition in such summary fashion?

My students preface my name with the title "Doctor," but I try not to let it get to me and distort my awareness of just how little my mind can ever really know. Human nutrition is incredibly complex. It's simply impossible for science today even to begin to understand its many ramifications. We are aware of only a small fraction of the vast quantity of nutritional needs.

Fortunately, these needs do not require thought. If they did, the human race would be as extinct as the dinosaurs. Eat what your appetite tells you it wants, but stay away from modern perversions of food.

133. What do you eat?

I try to eat a variety of fresh fruits and vegetables. Variety is important, because the nutrition that is not in one food might be in another. I don't care for too much meat, although I'm not a vegetarian. I like milk, yogurt and cheese.

I eat bread sparingly. In the summer, I consume large quantities of a variety of fruit juices including apple, grape, orange and pineapple juice.

I do not use salt at the table or at the stove.

I do not use sugar, because it seems to make my skin break out in acne. Also, sugar dulls my taste to the sensitive flavors of more bland foods. Only rarely will I eat cake, pie, ice cream or candy.

134. Why don't you use salt?

There are three reasons:

1. It is unnecessary to salt one's food, because there are traces of salt that appear naturally in a variety of foods.

This is all that my body needs. The salt concentration of the body fluids is very accurately regulated and does not vary from individual to individual. Your body fluids contain the same concentration of salt as mine, even if you use the salt shaker liberally. My body conserves its salt, while yours must work to excrete the excess.

2. Salt masks the natural flavor of foods. This makes it difficult for the appetite to guide one in the selection of needed foods.

3. Eating excess salt places an additional strain on the circulatory system. Isn't salt the first restriction given patients with high blood pressure or other circulatory ailments? With less strain from excess salt, the circulatory system is free to apply more effort to running.

135. Isn't extra salt necessary, especially in hot weather?

Yes and no. This requires a detailed explanation.

The average American diet is excessively high in salt. Salt acts like an addictive drug. Once you get used to having it in excess, you suffer withdrawal symptoms if you are deprived of it. Thus, when the average person works in the heat and sweats excessively, he takes salt tablets in order to replace the salt lost in the sweat. If he does not get additional salt, he suffers withdrawal symptoms of nausea and muscle cramps.

If one does not use table salt and is not addicted, then extra salt is unnecessary even when running in the heat. Such a runner has very little salt in his sweat compared to the average person. His body has learned to conserve the salt it needs.

Therefore, runners who salt their food liberally will need even more salt in the summer months. Those who are used to a low-salt diet need not concern themselves with extra salt, which would in fact upset their systems.

136. Do you recommend that every runner go on a low-salt diet?

Going on a low-salt diet will not make you a champion

runner. It will improve the efficiency of your circulatory system and make you somewhat faster in races, especially under very hot conditions. The runner must decide for himself whether a small increase in performance level is worth the loss of the salty flavor he loves.

137. I want to go on a low-salt diet. How can I do it without getting muscle cramps?

If you are used to salting your food, then you should not start the low-salt diet during the summer. The lack of salt that your body is accustomed to having can cause muscle cramps and nausea. Simply wait until the cold winter months, then throw the salt shaker away. By the time summer returns, you should be free of the salt habit. You will surprised as to how much easier summer running becomes.

If you live in a climate that is warm year-round, then you will have to reduce gradually the amount of salt used.

138. How did you arrive at these ideas concerning salt?

In the winter of 1967, I was living alone and stopped using salt for the simple reason that I kept forgetting to buy it at the supermarket. Prior to this time, I had always had considerable difficulty racing in the high heat and humidity which characterize the summers in the northeast.

The National AAU Marathon Championship was staged in Holyoke, Mass., on June 11, 1967, and was also the selection race for the Pan-American Games team. The conditions were unbelievable. The race started at noon under a clear sky with both the temperature and the humidity in the high 90s. As America's best marathoners awaited the starter's pistol, they found their feet sticking lightly to the softening asphalt road.

Only 30 of the original 125 starters made it to the finish of this race which became known later as the "Great Holyoke Massacre." I finished fourth, beating many runners who were far better at the marathon. I was delighted with my performance and even more delighted with my discovery of the effects of my low-salt diet.

Immediately after the race, I spoke to Ted Corbitt, one of the most experienced runners of all time. I told him of my low-salt diet and how I thought it had aided me this day. Ted is a quiet fellow who never laughs, but my words brought a rare grin to his normally stone-like face.

He replied, "I haven't used salt for that reason since the 1950s."

Since that experience I have never used the salt shaker at the dinner table or at the stove. My wife and two sons also never use salt. One day, while visiting friends, my six-year-old son Eric tried a few salted nuts from an available candy dish. He immediately choked and cried, "Ehh . . . Daddy! What is this!" He had tasted salt for the first time.

139. Can long-distance runners get fat?

They can frequently gain 10, 20 or 30 pounds of fat even though they continue to train. The runner only burns about 100 calories in each mile of running. It makes little difference whether he runs fast or slow, he still burns about 100 calories per mile. To lose one pound of fat requires a deficiency of about 3500 calories in the runner's diet. This means that the runner must travel 35 miles just to lose one pound of fat!

Since it's far easier to eat 3500 calories than it is to run 35 miles, many runners find it easy to gain unwanted weight. I know this all too well, for I have at times gained 25 pounds over the winter months when my interest in running generally declines.

140. If I gain a few pounds of excess fat, will I slow down in races?

Very definitely, yes! Every pound of unneeded weight has a measurable effect in the runner's final time. From my own experience, I estimate that I lose two seconds per mile run for each excess pound of body fat.

For example, if I gain five pounds, then I lose 10 seconds for each mile of the race. If the race is 10 miles long, I run slower by 100 seconds or one minute and 40 seconds. Obviously, this is a considerable decrease in performance. The following table gives a more extensive idea of the effect of excess weight:

TIME LOST IN RACING DUE TO EXCESS BODY WEIGHT

Race	Pounds of Excess Fat			
Distance	1 lb.	5 lbs.	10 lbs.	20 lbs.
5 miles	10 sec.	50 sec.	1:40	3:20
10 miles	20 sec.	1:40	3:20	6:40
20 miles	40 sec.	3:20	6:40	13:20
Marathon	52-sec.	4:20	8:40	17:20
50 miles	1:40	8:20	16:40	33:20

141. How do you lose weight?

With aggravating difficulty. I have never been able to lose significant weight by increasing my training mileage. Some lucky runners can, but I seem to be too efficient. Rather, I must restrict my caloric input. I find this far harder than the most severe racing and training. Unfortunately, it is necessary if I wish to race well.

142. What weight-reduction diets have you tried? Which do you recommend?

Since I have an unfortunate history as a "fatty," I have had the opportunity to try several diets. These include:

1. Eating very little of a variety of everyday foods.

2. The high-protein diet. Here, one eats only meat, eggs and cottage cheese in any quantity desired.

3. The low-carbohydrate diet. Here, one eats foods high in protein and fat, but very low in carbohydrates. The quantity of food is restricted.

4. The juice-fast diet. Here, one eats no solid food but drinks liberal quantities of fruit juices at will.

I only recommend the first diet, which is also the simplest. The variety of foods eaten tends to make me feel better. I suppose there is less nutritional deficiency with this diet.

143. Describe your dieting procedure in detail. How rapidly do you lose weight?

I begin by getting very, very small bowls and dishes from which to eat. I prepare a variety of foods, anything I like, but I only allow myself to eat the small quantity that I can fit in my tiny bowl. I do not eat between meals. I drink diluted fruit juice or water.

When training, I usually do short, hard runs. These tend to tie up my stomach and cause me to lose my appetite. I have a small treat before bed so that I can get to sleep.

Since I eat very little in this way, I usually lose about one pound of body weight per day.

144. Do you restrict your fluid intake when dieting?

Absolutely not! This would be very foolish and very dangerous. I drink all the diluted fruit juice I like.

I once restricted my fluid intake, and found that I developed an eye condition known as central serositis. It was very frightening, and I am very fortunate that the condition passed after about two months. I believe that fluid restriction is the most dangerous trick one can attempt while dieting.

145. Do you reduce your training mileage while dieting?

Only if I feel too weak to run my normal mileage. Even with a very serious reduction in food intake, I can usually run. But I do find that I feel weary for most of the workout.

146. How long do you continue your diet?

The first few days of the diet are very difficult. I become very irritable and find that I lose patience quickly with my family and friends. I become very unpleasant. After about one week, I no longer feel hungry, and my personality improves. After two weeks, I begin to feel better in my workouts. I continue the diet until I lose the necessary weight, which is usually about three weeks.

147. Can you race well while dieting?

No. You can enter races, but your times will be very slow. In long races, you probably won't be able to finish. However, once you return to normal eating, your racing performances will pick up with astonishing speed. I only require 24 hours of normal eating to run a good race following a very hard diet.

148. Isn't your diet too hard on your body? Wouldn't it be better to lose the weight more slowly?

Yes, it probably is too hard. I only do it because I find at times I am very anxious to get back into good racing form. It would be better to lose the weight gradually, say one or two pounds per week. Unfortunately, I've never had the patience to do this effectively.

9

HOT, COLD
AND WET

149. What weather is ideal for producing fast racing times?

For relatively short races, say up to 10 miles, still, clear 50-degree air is very comfortable. In longer races, dehydration becomes a problem, and thus colder air is needed. I like a clear, still day at about 30 degrees for the marathon, and 20 degrees is even better for a 50-miler.

This might at first appear to be too cold, but in these very long races, most runners are losing incredible quantities of body fluid, and this becomes a critical factor in the final miles of the race. The very cold air prevents this water loss.

A word should be said for the merits of a cold rain. I ran my fastest marathon in 1967 at Boston when the temperature was 35 degrees and a cold rain chilled us most of the way. I felt very uncomfortable, but I ran like hell, and I owe my 2:29:04 performance to this rain.

On very cold or rainy days, young and inexperienced runners have a chance to defeat their more experienced opponents because they do not have to worry about saving themselves in the early stages of the race. They can run fast from the gun, and the cold air prevents them from dehydrating. On warmer days they would pay severely for their imprudent early speed.

I have watched many young runners produce a remarkably fast time in their first marathon on cold or wet days, and then wonder why they can't repeat the performance when the weather is warmer.

A recent example is Jim Pearson's victory in the National AAU 50-Mile Championship in October 1975. It was Pearson's first race at 50 miles, and he went out at record speed. A cold, bone-piercing rain tortured the runners for the entire distance, and when Pearson crossed the finish line in 5:12:40 he had two miles on America's greatest ever 50-miler, Max White, and a new American record.

150. What weather condition is most dangerous for racing?

Cold weather is uncomfortable, but hot weather literally kills. Deaths in long races are very rare, but when they do

Osler in the late stages of a track 50. (Photo by Ed Dodd)

occur, they almost always fall on very hot, humid days. The oppressive one-two punch of heat and humidity is common during the summers in the eastern United States. All too often, I have watched runners, even well-conditioned ones, nearly kill themselves. In 1961, in a race in Reader, W. Va., two boys actually died.

Even if the temperature is not very high, say 75 degrees, a blazing noonday sun can also kill. Runners often say that the sun is their worst enemy. It literally cooks the brain.

151. Have you ever seen world-class runners collapse in the heat?

Yes, in the 1959 USA vs. USSR track meet, three of the four starters in the 10,000-meter run collapsed. The race was held at the famed Franklin Field in Philadelphia.

It started at noon, under a clear July sun with humid, hot, still air. You could cut the tension with a knife as the four starters walked to the line. For America, there was Bob Soth and Max Truex; for Russia, Hubert Pyarnakivi and Aleksey Desyatchikov. These were the Cold War days, and it mattered little that the Americans' best performances were a solid minute slower than their Russian opponents'; American are supposed to have guts, and we don't like losers.

The pace was as hot as the sun, 4:30 for the mile and 9:15 for two. Quickly, Truex dropped off the pace and ran to survive while Soth hung onto the two Russian pacesetters. At three miles, Soth began the strangest performance I have ever witnessed. He slowed to a gentle trot and began to weave across all the lanes of the track. He hit the curb and fell in what looked like slow motion onto the infield.

The officials foolishly urged him to return to the track. He rose, now moving limply like a rag doll. He started on his way again, only he was circling the track in the wrong direction. His head was thrown backward, his eyes looking at the sky. He fell after a few more steps and was immediately rushed to the hospital.

Next, it was the Russian Pyarnakivi's turn. He was 120 yards from the finish line, but he too began to run as though in a trance like Soth. His body leaned backward and his eyes appeared to search the sky. With less than 100 yards to go, he was moving slower than a walker.

Max Truex, who had been conserving his energy and had been lapped by this Russian, suddenly realized that he might be able to beat him—even though he had to make up a full lap. The crowd went wild as Truex passed the Russian and began his incredible task of running 540 yards before the Russian went 100.

Never have I witnessed so exciting a contest, Truex madly dashing around the first, then the second turn as Pyarnakivi weirdly did his unconscious dance on the homestretch. As Truex left the final curve with 50 yards remaining, the Russian appeared motionless five yards from the tape. Truex charged down the straight and passed Pyarnakivi just before he fell across the finish line. Both men were then rushed to the hospital to join Soth.

While everyone was watching the intense drama unfolding on the track, the officials lost count of the laps. Poor Aleksey Desyatchikov protested as the officials insisted that he go yet another lap. Fortunately, he was in good condition, and he won the race without the need for medical help.

152. If even great runners can collapse in the heat, should races continue to be run under such dangerous conditions?

As with all things, the danger lies not in the weather conditions themselves but in the ignorance of the runners. With proper care, all four of the runners would have finished without undue harm and would have made a valid competitive race out of their performances.

Heat, like cold, altitude and hills, is a naturally occurring condition. It adds to the great variety of circumstances under which we race. Some run well in the heat, some run badly—such is sport.

I see no more reason to cancel hot-day races than I do to objections that a particular course might be too long. Why not shorten the marathon to 20 miles so that we won't strain over those last tough six?

153. How can you tell if the weather is sufficiently warm to slow the runner's performance?

The simplest test I know does not even involve using a thermometer. It is the starting-line test. If you feel comfortable standing at the starting line in your shorts then it is too warm for racing at your fastest possible pace. The longer the distance of the race, the greater is the need for caution, even on a mildly warm day. Certainly, at the marathon distance mild warmth will cause many runners to quit.

154. How should I protect myself in a hot-day race?

The symptoms that precede heat exhaustion are rather mild and this makes hot-day racing most dangerous. These symptoms include mild headache, dizziness and nausea. If any of these are noticed to even the slightest degree, you should stop and walk, or quit the race. It may be your last warning before you collapse and possibly die. Another very dangerous sign occurs when you cease sweating. The skin becomes flushed and very warm to touch. Again, stop and sit down in the shade.

Further musts include:

1. Start very, very slowly. Once you get overheated from too fast a pace, you've blown the race. You can't drop your body temperature by slowing down later. You will have to stop altogether.

2. Take all the cold water you can get and pour it over your head, neck, chest, shoulders, arms and back. I can run a fast 50-mile track race under a hot, 90-degree, humid sun if I have my "rain machine." This is a tub of ice water filled with large sponges. Every 2-4 laps, I grab a sponge and drench myself while running. I look like I just emerged from a swimming pool. The ice water cools the body and prevents the need for excess sweating which in turn leads to dehydration.

3. If the race is really long, say more than 20 miles, it will be necessary to drink fluids. I drink about one gallon of sugared iced tea during a 50-mile race under very hot conditions.

155. What is the best drink to take during a hot race?

I have experimented with most of the available commercial drinks designed for this purpose and have concluded that they are all inferior to the drinks I prefer: iced tea and orange juice, both mixed with plenty of sugar.

156. I read that sugar in the drink will retard its ability to pass through the stomach. Is this true?

My personal experience is not in agreement with the physiologists. I have mixed up to an entire two-pound box of sugar in a one gallon container of iced tea and consumed it all in a 50-mile race without difficulty.

However, I suggest you try this in training for yourself before you try it in an important race. I find that the sugar gives me an immediate lift which I can't get otherwise during the late stages of a race.

I wish to note here that I do *not* recommend the use of sugar at any time except during a long race. I think of sugar as a strong drug and use it only during the most strenuous activity.

157. How much fluid should I drink in a race?

This can be calculated with reasonable accuracy. In training, weigh yourself before and after the workout. Determine how many pounds were lost, and then divide this into the number of miles run. This will tell you how many miles are run before one pound of body fluid is lost through sweat. For example, if you run 16 miles and lose four pounds, then you have run 16/4 = 4 miles for every pound of water lost.

Now suppose you are going to race 50 miles under similar conditions. You lose one pound of water for every four miles of running, thus you will lose about 50/4 = 12.5 pounds of fluid in the race. A runner weighing about 140 pounds can lose about four pounds of water without difficulty, but 12 pounds would be fatal.

You must therefore drink at least eight pounds of water during the race. One quart of water weighs two pounds.

Thus, you must drink 8/2 = 4 quarts of fluid during the race. This is a great deal, but it must be done. Even then you will suffer a four-pound loss after the race.

158. How can you consume that much fluid during a race?

Drink small quantities, frequently. For example, I drink about 12 ounces every half-hour during a very long race.

159. Will training in hot weather acclimatize me to the heat?

Only to a small degree. You must use your head and protect yourself at all times. You can never, never run with a sense of abandon that you use on cool days. No heroics, please! All that being gutsy will get you is a quick trip to the emergency room of the nearest hospital.

After living and training for two weeks in sultry weather, your body will have acclimatized to the small degree that it can.

160. What adjustments should be made to my training during hot weather?

The most important aspect of hot-weather training is to keep out of the sun. Train in the coolest part of the day—mornings and evenings, but never under the mid-day sun. I can frequently endure heat and humidity in the absence of direct sunlight.

161. How can I get used to the heat if I don't train in it?

Most runners make the mistake of thinking that by training in the heat of the day they will condition themselves to race in it. This is folly. All that training in the heat will do is make you weary and worn out.

Running under the hot sun is like being hit with a stick. You can't get accustomed to being beaten by a stick, you only emerge as a pulp. So it is with those who insist on training under the sun on hot, humid days.

162. Have you ever seen a runner from a cold climate win a hot-day race?

Yes. A runner from a cold climate has an advantage over those who have been forced to train day after day under oppressively hot conditions—if he knows how to use his advantage. He must start slowly and build into the race.

The 1967 National AAU Marathon Championship and Pan-American Games Trial mentioned earlier became an unforgettable classic known now as the "Great Holyoke Massacre." It was humid and hot, and the race started under a clear noonday sun. The leaders went out at a blistering pace. The eventual winner, Ron Daws, started slowly from the back of the field of 125 runners and after many miles of running assumed the lead. Most of the good runners, who had trained in the heat, quit. Daws, from Minnesota, had not run in weather warmer than 50 degrees. He won because he kept his head and because he was fresh.

Later, Daws claimed that he had acclimatized to the heat by training in multiple sweatsuits. But the tremendous drain on the runners' reserves created by running in very hot and humid weather cannot be simulated in cool weather by wearing extra clothing. The very air we breathe here on the East Coast is stifling in the summer and makes everyone very lethargic.

163. What should I wear while training in very hot weather?

I prefer nylon trunks. Both nylon and cotton running shirts are available, and I like wearing both. My shoes fit well, and thus I do not need socks. Unless you have a good thick head of hair, a hat should be worn if the sun is overhead. I always wear a comfortable sun visor. It serves as both a sweat band and as an eye shield when the sun is low. Too much sun should be avoided as it is bad for the skin.

164. Can I train and race in very cold weather?

Yes. The cold temperatures offer little problem. The primary difficulty comes from the ice and snow that usually accompany very cold conditions.

165. What should I wear when training in cold weather?

You do not have to wear a great deal of clothing to keep warm. Here are a few tricks I've learned over the years:

1. Place a thin plastic bag (such as that used by dry cleaners) between your undershirt and your sweatshirt. This will keep your body heat from escaping and also keep the wind's bite out.

2. Most runners prefer long, tight underwear to sweat pants.

3. It is very important for men to protect the genitals. These can freeze easily if you run many miles into the wind. For this purpose, you must wear a pair of wind-proof nylon trunks to hold in body heat. I once saw a runner wear cotton shorts in an 18-mile race during a snowstorm. When he finished, his penis felt frozen and he was in great pain. This is an experience you don't want. If nylon trunks are not available, then place a piece of thin plastic wrap over this area.

4. The breathing of very cold air might become a problem for some runners. One solution is to wear a mask or cloth over the mouth and nose. Incoming air is warmed by the heat left in the mask by the previously exhaled air.

5. To balance out the difference in chill factor between running into and against the wind, it's a good idea to wear adjustable clothing. This can be achieved with layers of light clothing. For example, a light nylon wind-breaker can be tied around the waist when running with the wind.

6. Growing a beard helps to keep the face warm when running into the wind.

7. A good hat and gloves round out the runner's attire.

166. What shoes can be used for running in snow?

Nylon shoes are not good. Leather is better because it is waterproof to a degree. Leather shoes can become very stiff and hard from snow running. Cover them with petroleum jelly; this will keep the water out of the leather and help keep it soft.

I wear socks in the winter to keep my feet warm. If the snow is melting, the feet will freeze from ice water soaking through the shoes unless special precautions are taken. Place a thin cotton sock on the foot. Then place a plastic bag over the thin sock. Finally, either put another sock over the plastic bag, or place your foot directly into the shoe. The bag will keep the water from reaching your skin.

167. What weather do you prefer for training?

I prefer warm weather. I like the summer months, even though it is very hot and humid in New Jersey where I live. I like the feel of the sun and the air on my bare skin.

Many runners, however, prefer cold weather. Everyone runs faster in the cold, because the body is not fighting to keep its temperature from boiling over. One can run faster and farther in the cold months than in the hot summer.

PART THREE
Racing Quickly

10
TECHNIQUES AND TACTICS

168. Is racing good for one's health?

I am a veteran of over 750 long-distance races, and I can't imagine one of these that did my general health any good. Racing is simply too hard to be placed in the healthful exercise category.

Nevertheless, if it were not for my interest in racing, I probably would have abandoned my training runs long ago. These training runs have been an enormous boon to my general well-being, both physical and mental. Thus, for many runners, racing is an indirect blessing. It keeps them interested in staying fit.

With knowledge and common sense, the dangers of racing can be made minimal. In spite of the high stress created by long-distance racing, those who compete regularly over a period of many years enjoy far more robust health than their inactive neighbors.

169. Should young children run long-distance races?

No. Few adults are able to evaluate the intensity of their racing efforts so as to avoid injury. How can we expect this from children? It is the duty of the mature and experienced to protect the young. Often, this means forbidding them to partake in events that they want very much to experience.

A reasonable degree of physical maturity should be reached before even the semblance of training begins. The numerical age at which it becomes safe to run seriously varies from individual to individual. Certainly, the young athlete should have passed through puberty. Perhaps 13 is the earliest age that should be tolerated for entry into a long-distance race.

Often, those who support the entry of youngsters point to the experience of swimmers. In swimming, they sometimes begin training earlier than age five. But running is not swimming. The swimmer does not fight gravity. With every step, the runner absorbs more than his body's weight through the bones and tendons of the foot and leg. These powerful forces are the cause of the many injuries so common in running.

Growing children should be free of such unnatural abuse. I have two sons of my own, and you won't find them in long-distance races until they are fully grown.

170. Should women run long-distance races?

Women are well suited to endurance activities. In general, the average woman cannot develop the muscular strength of her male counterpart, but she can develop her cardio-respiratory system. Since distance running is largely a question of cardio-respiratory efficiency, women can compete at all distances.

In every race, muscular strength is a factor. But as the races get longer, the importance of muscular strength diminishes. For this reason, the woman runner will probably always be somewhat slower than the male, although the difference should diminish as the distance of the race increases.

171. Should I run "all-out" in every race?

Not if you desire to have a running career lasting several decades. The mature runner must learn to control the intensity of his racing efforts. At the right time, when he is well trained, he can race all-out, but this should be infrequent. He should learn how to run an "easy race."

172. Exactly how frequently should I allow myself to race "all-out"?

In general, the longer the race, the greater is the degree of fatigue endured by the runner. As a rule of thumb, *for well-trained runners* it takes about one day for each mile of the race for complete recovery. This means that it takes five days to recover from a five-miler, 10 days for a 10-miler and one month for the marathon. The runner will require longer periods of recovery if he is not thoroughly trained.

You might feel that these recovery times are too long, because you will probably feel quite well in workouts long before this recovery time elapses. This is deceiving. You feel good, but there is still deep, residual fatigue. You would discover this were you to race all-out again and find that your legs went flat in the final miles.

I believe the runner should *double* the above-mentioned recovery time before he attempts another all-out performance. This means that he should wait 10 days after a five-mile race, 20 days after a 10-miler and two months after a marathon before he attempts another all-out race. If he chooses to race sooner than this, he should make it a controlled "easy effort."

In the case of very long races, even longer recovery times should be adopted. This will be discussed later.

173. What is the effect of starting too fast or too slow in a race?

Here are the effects of three different methods of varying the pace during a race:

1. *Start fast, then gradually slow down in the later stages of the race.* This is the pacing employed by over 90% of the runners in most races. It is particularly common in high school and college runs. This is the most fatiguing and uncomfortable way to run, because an early oxygen debt is created which the runner then carries until the race is concluded. The final time is slower than the runner can produce. The degree of fatigue is deep.

2. *Run the entire race at a steady pace.* This method of pacing, at least in theory, should produce the fastest time possible by the runner. Only the most experienced runners seem able to judge the pace correctly under racing conditions. The degree of fatigue created is large, but not as large as that produced by starting too fast.

3. *Start slowly and gradually accelerate throughout the race.* Very few runners employ this tactic. The final time produced is not as fast as can be achieved with steady speed, but the degree of overall fatigue is less. This is the easiest way to run a race as it produces the least post-race weariness.

174. How do you run an "easy race"?

The goal in running an easy race is to produce a relatively fast performance (though not as fast as possible) without creating deep fatigue. To do this, the runner should start the race quite slowly and only gradually accelerate the pace. Here are specific details of the method I employ:

1. First, I divide the distance of the race into three equal parts. For example, a six-miler is thought of as three consecutive two-mile components, a marathon is three nine-mile segments. Each component is run according to a very different plan.

2. During the first third of the race, I imagine that I am not racing at all. I start quite gently, and everyone seems to be running away from me. Frequently, I am in last place. I think gentle thoughts and never challenge anyone. Anytime a runner moves up to my shoulder, I deliberately slow down and let him pass. I remain as unconcerned and casual as possible.

3. During the second third of the race, I continue coasting at the slow pace of the first third, but I now run several mildly-fast bursts at selected points. I look down the road about 200-300 yards and identify a particular marker such as a tree or a building. I then pick up the pace until I reach that marker, after which I return to the easy pace. I move rather fast during these segments but not so fast as to get fatigued. I usually pass several runners this way, as they

are not expecting such accelerations at this point in the race.

4. During the final third of the race, I open up and run home with a quick, steady speed to the finish line. If I've run the two previous segments correctly, I feel like a wild animal let loose. I pass runners left and right. I feel a great sense of exhilaration as I am so fresh that no one I catch can put up a serious challenge.

175. Should I stop running several days before a race?

Before running a hard race, you certainly should allow time for your body to rest so that it will be thoroughly free of any fatigue generated by training. However, I find it best not to stop training completely.

I have been running for so many years that my body requires a certain level of activity in order to function smoothly. When I don't run, my digestion is upset, my bowels do not move properly, and my sleep is interrupted. Thus, I prefer to run a few easy miles during the two or three days before a hard race.

176. What should I eat before a race?

There are two considerations:

1. Don't eat any solid food within four hours of the start. This will be in your system and may cause stomach cramps. You can drink small quantities of fluid up to 30 minutes before the gun.

2. The night before and the morning of the race, eat foods to which you are accustomed and which are digested easily. *Do not eat anything you would not eat normally at these times.* It would be a mistake, for instance, to have eggs for breakfast if you never eat them otherwise. I find that carbohydrates are most easily digested. Thus, I have noodles and salad for dinner, and cake and tea for breakfast.

177. How should I travel to the race?

Always use the most comfortable means of transportation

available. If I can't afford to fly to a race that is more than 200 miles away, I usually won't go at all. I find any bus trip longer than two hours too fatiguing. If you are going by car, try to have a non-runner do the driving. Runners get a nervous adrenalin build-up before the race. This takes their concentration off of driving and makes them accident-prone.

If you are driving more than 50 miles to the race, it is important to stop the car and run easily for 5-10 minutes at least once each hour. This will keep your digestion working and keep your legs from going stiff. Plan to leave so that you arrive at least 1-1½ hours before the starting time. You don't want to use up your nervous energy wondering if you'll be late.

178. Should I learn the route of the course before the race?

If you are a leading contender for top places in the race, you should make every effort to see the course beforehand and learn every turn. You can't rely on spotters doing their job at every turn. Race directors usually do their best to cover every turn, but they often lack sufficient volunteers to perform these tasks.

In 1969, the first three runners in the National AAU Marathon Championship went off course in the final few miles. The eventual winner was the man running fourth when the mishap occurred.

179. Are courses utilizing repeated small loops more difficult than those through more varied scenery?

Psychologically, most runners prefer to run from one point to another without ever retracing their steps. They find the changing landscape refreshing and an aid in forgetting the fatiguing effects of running.

However, in most areas it is very difficult to lay out a race course of this type. Traffic problems as well as the need to monitor the race often make it necessary to run the race over a small loop which the runners repeat many times to complete the full distance.

I know many marathon runners who complain that they can't run over repeated loops. They have allowed their minds to get the best of them. It is no more difficult to run 200 laps of a quarter-mile track than it is to run 50 miles from one city to the next. In fact, the 50-mile track race might be a great deal easier since refreshment is available every lap.

The great Australian coach Percy Cerutty once said, "A good runner can run anywhere." Racing over small loops is part of the sport, and good runners worth their salt learn to master it.

180. Does abstinence from sexual activity produce superior racing performances?

The concept that avoiding sexual activity will generate strength in the athlete dates back to ancient times. Walter Thom in his book *Pedestrianism* (1813) writes when describing the athletes of ancient Greece that "the sexual intercourse was strictly prohibited." As a boy in high school, I recall that these ideas were well circulated in locker-room conversation and they had a strong effect on me.

After years of personal experience, I conclude that there is absolutely no foundation to this concept. Sexual activity, like any other activity, can be done to excess, and the results will show in inferior athletic performance. But sexual activity at a frequency that is normal for the particular individual has no relation to running performance. I believe that it is far wiser for an athlete to have sexual activity the night before a major race than to lie in bed awake from the unreleased tension.

181. What should I do in the hour preceding the race?

Besides the obvious need to check in, go to the toilet and warm up, it is most important to stay alone and concentrate on the race at hand. There will be a large crowd of runners and officials. Many of them will be old friends, perhaps very close friends. On any other occasion, you would want to renew your friendships and converse liberally. Now, you must dispense with these customs in the briefest manner that courtesy allows and remain quiet. You can burn up a great deal of energy standing and talking.

I like to find a quiet, secluded corner where I lie down and concentrate on the job at hand. In a short time, I will be locked in a desperate struggle against the clock and these many friendly faces. I try to relax and not lose control of myself as the adrenalin now floods my system. The tension mounts. I usually urinate several times.

Finally, I warm up about 15 minutes before being called to the start. I ask God's forgiveness for the abuse I am about to subject on this body he has temporarily entrusted to my care.

182. What should I do at the start?

If you are a leading contender and the field is large, you should be in the front row. You can lose considerable time by starting behind a large group of runners. If the running path is wide open and you do not envision any bottlenecks on the course at which you will be unable to pass runners, then try to settle down to a steady speed as quickly as possible.

When the gun fires, you need to move off the line quickly for a few steps to avoid being stepped on, but you should then settle quickly into the appropriate speed. Since nearly everyone runs the first mile of the race far too fast, you will find yourself quite far back. There is no worry; fast starters more than pay for their folly later.

You will not be able to start at a steady speed if the running path quickly narrows and prevents you from passing. In this case, you have no choice but to move out fast.

183. How does it feel to run the race at steady speed?

After many races and time-trials, the body learns how to fall into the appropriate speed for the race. I feel as though I am running quite slowly in the early stages of the race.

Gradually, I seem to be going faster and faster. The final miles seem like a desperate rush to the finish line.

Of course, this is all an illusion, for I am in reality running at a steady pace. I only feel as though I'm going faster and faster because fatigue is overtaking my body.

184. Should I adjust my pace to the intermediate times I hear called?

In general, this is unwise. It is far better to let your body instinctively dictate the appropriate pace. The exact ideal pace for the conditions cannot be calculated beforehand. It is not possible to measure the effect of temperature, hills, wind, footing, etc.

I don't quite know how it does it, but my body can sense the appropriate pace for the moment and the particular conditions prevailing. I have run 10-mile track races where the lap times were recorded but not called to the runners. After the race, I am usually amazed at how steady my pace was. The laps from beginning to end often did not vary by more than three seconds.

185. Should I talk during the race?

An occasional word or two does no harm, but continuous conversation will certainly affect your performance. Talking reduces the ability of the lungs to handle oxygen, and the result will be a slower final time.

186. What should I do immediately upon crossing the finish line?

It is important to keep warm and to cool down gradually. Immediately put on warm clothes, then begin slow jogging and brisk walking. This should continue for 10-15 minutes before stopping. By keeping the circulation rapid, you help the body remove the waste products of fatigue. If it is cold, get inside as soon as you have completed the cool-down. Don't stand in the cold air and talk.

187. How will I feel in the days following the race?

After a very hard long race, stiffness in the thighs is usually felt in the morning after the race. It often grows worse during the day. On the second and third days, the soreness intensifies. You have difficulty walking down stairs. You appreciate how it feels to be 90 years old. On the fourth and fifth days, the stiffness often quickly subsides.

The degree of leg stiffness endured after racing will depend on the length of the race and the thoroughness of your base training. I do not get stiff from races shorter than 10 miles. If the race is very hilly, I am usually left quite sore afterward compared to a flat race of the same length.

Following a hard effort, the body's overall resistance to colds and other infections is reduced. Appropriate care should be taken.

188. Should I train on the day following a hard race?

Yes, but the degree of fatigue you endured must dictate the program of the workout. I can usually resume normal training on the day following a hard race shorter than 10 miles. It might be a week before I feel ready for regular training following a marathon.

Mild activity aids the body in the recovery process. Following the very hardest races, when the legs are quite stiff and sore, brisk walking for one or two hours is restorative.

189. Do runners get very hungry following hard races?

Immediately after a very hard racing effort, the stomach is simply too tired to digest food, and most runners will eat only sparingly. However, on the days following the race, the runner's appetite is likely to climb considerably above normal. I find this true particularly after very long races.

It is very easy to gain weight at an alarmingly rapid rate. I find it necessary to carefully control my eating habits so as not to put on excessive amounts of fat that will have to be worked off later. The combination of reduced training and ravishing appetite often results in a five-pound weight gain in just one week.

190. When are tactical considerations useful in distance running?

Tactical considerations are of importance only when the competitors concerned are at very nearly the same performance level. You can't very well apply tactics to a competitor who is not within easy reach.

191. What is the basic principle around which all tactics center?

You try to discourage your opponents by making them feel that they have no hope of beating you.

In every distance race, there comes a period when all the runners are very weary. No longer do their bodies drive forward easily. Rather, their steps become reluctant, and each runner must use his will-power to keep the pace rapid. This phase is quite noticeable after three-fourths of the race distance is covered. It is at this stage of the race that clever tactics can be most effective.

For example, if you pass an opponent looking strong and running easily, you might make him think that there is no hope for him to beat you. Once these negative thoughts are planted in his mind, his pace will likely slacken and you have him beaten.

192. Can you illustrate how you have used such tactics?

The National AAU Championship at 30 kilometers took place on a sunny, warm day in March 1967. Looking over the field, I realized there were three runners who were very much better than I at this distance. The clear favorite was Lou Castagnola, who had recently established an American record for the two-hour run. However, it was sunny and 80 degrees. In hot weather, there is always a chance that the stars will blow up and fail to finish.

I started at a slow speed and by 12 miles found myself in second place. Castagnola was about one minute ahead. With three miles remaining, I drew even with Lou. The fact that I had been running faster than he made me hope that

I could fly past him. Unfortunately, he held on tenaciously. Lou has a much faster finish than I, and both of us knew that he would be the winner if we did not separate soon.

I studied Lou carefully. At this point in the race, the road was winding. As we ran from one side of the road to the other in order to run the shortest distance, I noticed that Lou accidentally brushed my shoulder several times. This meant that he was growing clumsy from fatigue. My confidence rose; I was convinced that I could take him.

Tom Osler during the AAU One-Hour Run in New Jersey in July of 1977 (7th place, 10m, 291y). (Photo by Ed Dodd)

There was a lead car about 10 yards in front of us. I knew that I must crush Lou's hope of winning. I looked at the driver and said, "I'm ready to run in to the finish now. Will you stay with me and show me the way?"

My outrageous confidence took Lou totally by surprise. I dashed forward almost at top speed and ran as though the devil were at my heels. I was afraid to look back. I had to convince Lou that I was going to keep this insane pace up to the finish. Fortunately, my trick worked and he immediately decelerated. I struggled as best I could to the finish line and won by three minutes.

Three weeks later, Lou proved that he had been the better man. He ran 2:17, taking fourth place in the Boston Marathon, while I finished 12 minutes later.

193. How can I develop a fast finishing kick?

The ability to sprint at the finish of a long race can be developed by appropriate psychological conditioning. It must be made a reflex action. In training, set up an imaginary area in which a race is finishing. Place a marker about 100 yards from the finish line. Every time you run by this marker, you sprint for all you're worth to the finish line. Soon, sprinting will be a reflex action, and you will be able to kick the final 100 yards of a race in spite of your fatigue.

I personally have ignored this aspect of racing. My natural sprinting speed is very slow. My fastest 100 yards is 14 seconds and my fastest 440 is 64 seconds. I have, therefore, developed what I call the sustained finish. I start a mild build-up about one mile from the finish line and hope to break my competitors before the final kicking range is reached.

194. Must I train on hills if I wish to race well in hilly races?

No. I have lived in southern New Jersey for most of my life. Here, it is difficult to find a hill worthy of the name. Yet I found that I could race over the hilliest courses and hold my own.

195. Should I run hard up the hills in races?

Many runners practice blasting every hill they see in training. This conditions them to do the same in racing. I do not believe this to be wise. I takes far more energy to gain five yards while going uphill than it does on the flat. Therefore, ground gained in this manner is gained at a high price.

196. How do you take the hills?

I like to run fast when the opposition is relaxing. When I race over a hill, I try to exert the same energy while going up the hill as I do while running on the flat. This means that I slow down when I cover a hill. Many runners, therefore, overtake me on the hill.

At the very crest of a hill, most runners falter. They can't wait to let up. Consequently, I spurt at the very top of a hill, and often make up the ground lost. I run hard downhill, because I have learned to relax and coast down hill at a fast pace.

Runners also flounder at the very bottom of a hill. Here again, I deliberately spurt in order to catch them by surprise.

11
RACING
3-20 MILES

197. Why have you included races in the wide range from 3-20 miles in one chapter?

There is a common feature shared by distance races shorter than 20 miles that is not found in longer races. They can be completed without emptying the runner's gas tank. In races longer than 20 miles, runners often "hit the wall," a syndrome in which the runner suddenly feels completely depleted and is often forced to a standstill. This rarely happens in shorter races. To overcome this syndrome requires considerable training over an extended period of time.

With relatively little training, gifted runners can race remarkably well over this range, but they will not succeed at the marathon unless they do far more training. A clear example of this is the case of my good friend Browning Ross.

Ross rarely ran more than 25 miles per week, yet he made both the 1948 and '52 Olympic teams in the steeplechase. He won major national and international championships at all distances from 1500 meters to 20 miles. Yet Ross always failed at the marathon. Twenty-five miles per week in training simply was not enough.

198. Is it important to run at a steady pace in these races?

It is only by running the race at a steady speed that the runner can hope to produce his best final time. Most runners, however, will run the first part of the race far faster than their average speed, and the consequences of such poor pacing will not be all that severe. The runner will most likely finish the race without undue difficulty, although he will slow down in the final stages. The price paid for poor pacing will not be great.

199. Do these races usually start too fast?

Yes, especially high school and college races. Young runners are often very psyched up before a race, and their lack of experience causes them to bolt out like a herd of wild animals on a stampede.

200. If I started at the appropriate speed, I will be far back of the leaders. Will I be able to catch them later?

If you are a contender for top position in the race, you very definitely can catch those who started too fast. (Of course, I am assuming that the running path is sufficiently wide for you to pass the runners in groups when the appropriate time arrives.)

Yes, you definitely have the physical ability to gradually work your way through the field and emerge victorious, but it usually takes experience to execute steady pacing effectively. Most novice runners lose heart when they see most of the field running away from them. They get nervous, their muscles tie up, and without relaxation their hopes of success are shattered.

The experienced runner, however, likes nothing better than to watch his opponent start far too fast. The rabbit-like starter will be all mush later in the race and easily beaten.

201. What is a cross-country race?

Strictly speaking, cross-country races are run over open fields, up and down hills, along forest paths, and even over fences and across little streams. These contrast with road races which are staged on the open road, where vehicular traffic ordinarily shares the course with the runner. Sometimes, however, a road race is advertised to be a cross-country race.

202. What special preparations are appropriate for cross-country racing?

Cross-country races are often very difficult. If at all possible, you should train on the very course on which you will race. This will allow you to master the most effective way to handle each of the obstacles on the course. Also, these courses are frequently difficult to follow, causing many competitors to get lost.

A runner is likely to find that bulky shoes that felt good on the track or on the road are not effective over the lumpy terrain on the cross-country course. He should experiment to see which shoes feel best on him.

Frequently, cross-country races are staged on very narrow trails through the woods on which it is nearly impossible to pass. This usually makes it imperative to discard steady pacing and go out fast at the gun.

203. What special preparations are needed for road racing?

Aside from thorough training for the distance to be run, the road racer must have shoes that will adequately absorb the shock of pounding on the hard road surface. He should experiment with various shoes until he finds the right compromise between light weight and an adequately thick, soft sole.

Road races differ from cross-country races in that they often require a hard, steady fast pace from start to finish. In cross-country racing, the various obstacles cause the pace to vary considerably—slow one moment, fast the next. This might upset the runner who is used to road racing.

204. Is vehicular traffic more dangerous when racing than when training?

It certainly is. Runners are fighting for every foot of ground and growing very tired and irritable. If the runner approaches an intersection in which he does not have the right of way, he is likely to dart out in front of a moving vehicle, assuming that the driver has brakes.

For this reason, every road runners' club should have a safety director who inspects the course before the race. This inspector should have the power to cancel the race if it cannot be made safe. I have run far too many road races that were unnecessarily dangerous.

Race promoters are not always to blame for unsafe courses. Part of the difficulty lies with the runners themselves. Runners become fond of their old courses, and courses that were fine 10 years ago might be very dangerous today.

When I became president of the Middle Atlantic Road Runners Club in 1968, I altered all the old, dangerous courses in our district. This sometimes meant that a 10-mile race course that had been one big loop was converted into several smaller, safe loops.

Before the start of one race, I heard someone say "let's take a vote. How many runners want to run the old course?" I held my ground. I told them that they could run anywhere they wished, but today's race was to be over the small loops. If they wanted to be part of the race, then they would run these and nothing else. Since no one else wanted to be president, I had no difficulty.

205. Is it necessary to train on a track in order to race long distances there?

No. Track racing is very much like road racing, particularly on the new all-weather surfaces. Many runners fear that they will find running many laps very monotonous, but this need not be the case.

I like to pretend I'm on the road when I enter track races, a road with many left hand turns! I concentrate on the developments in the race, and not on the laps or the lap times. When the lap times are called out, I often ignore them. This is easy when running, for it is difficult to make calculations mentally. I enjoy long track races. In particular, I like races of six and 10 miles and the one-hour run.

206. Why do you like long track races?

There are several reasons:

1. These races provide me with the opportunity to see accurately how well I can judge a steady pace. I try to have someone write down all my lap times. I study these very carefully later and see how the actual pace compared with my subjective sense of pace while running.

2. On a track, you have the opportunity to study other runners closely. Usually, the runners are spread all over the track with the fast ones lapping the slow many times. In a road race, you only get to see those who are just ahead of you.

3. In track races you don't worry about automobiles or dogs, and there is no chance of getting lost on the course!

207. How can you make sure that your laps are counted properly during a track race?

Even in a six-mile race, it is difficult for the runner to count his own laps as he circles the track. Yes, even counting to 24 is difficult when you are nearing exhaustion.

A simple method of double-checking your lap counter is to count the number of times the leader laps you. The winner's laps are almost always counted correctly. It is the also-rans who are often miscalculated. After the leader crosses the finish line to the applause of all present, you simply run as many more laps as the number of times you saw him overtake you.

RACING THE MARATHON

208. What is the marathon race?

The marathon race covers the distance of 26 miles, 385 yards and is almost always contested on the open road. It is the longest running event in the modern Olympic Games. In recent years, the marathon has become quite popular in the United States. Marathons are held all over the nation, at all times of the year, and they frequently draw 1000-5000 runners in a single race.

209. How did the marathon race originate?

The modern marathon commemorates the running feats of the ancient Greek herald Pheidippides. In 490 B.C., the Athenian Army defeated the Persians at a Greek town called Marathon. Legend has it that Pheidippides ran the 22 miles from the Plain of Marathon to Athens, gasped the words "rejoice, we conquer," then died on the spot.

The ancient historian Herodotus tells us that Pheidippides was no mean runner. Prior to the battle of Marathon, he was dispatched from Athens to Sparta to seek help. He ran the mountainous route of about 125 miles in one day. The Spartans were unable to offer the Athenians help for certain religious reasons.

As he ran back to Athens with the bad news, he fell in

with the god Pan, who called him by name. Pan offered the Athenians help provided that they ceased neglecting him. The Athenians believed this report. After the successful battle, they built a temple to Pan under the Acropolis and established in his honor yearly sacrifices and a torch race.

When the modern Olympic Games were revived in 1896 in Athens, the first marathon race was staged in memory of this event. It covered a distance of about 24 miles.

The 24-mile race at the Athens Olympics of 1896 was the first "marathon" race. Similar races began to spring up in other sporting nations. The first marathon held in the United States was in 1896 and was run from Stamford, Conn., to Columbus Circle in New York City.

210. What is the origin of the modern marathon distance?

The marathon race originated with and has remained in the modern Olympic Games. In 1896, the distance was only 24 miles. In 1906, again at Athens, the distance was increased to 26 miles.

In London, 1908, an Olympic marathon course of exactly 26 miles was established from the start on the lawn at Windsor Castle to the gate of the London stadium. Then, an additional 385 yards was added so that the race would finish in front of the Royal Box inside. The race has remained this length ever since.

211. Is it harder to race the marathon than 20 miles?

For most runners, it is much much harder. Most experienced marathoners say that the race begins at 20 miles and that the last six miles are harder than the first 20.

Most runners, after enjoying a few years of proper training, can run for 20 miles without exceptional difficulty. To go farther, however, seems to require much more training than would be expected. It seems that the energy available for running is all used up at about the 20-mile mark. The runner "hits the wall."

212. What does it feel like to "hit the wall" in the marathon?

It is an experience that must be felt to be appreciated. For the first 15 miles of the race, most runners are feeling relatively good. They are a bit tired but in good spirits. At about 18 miles, they begin to feel hungry; very, very hungry. Visions of ice cream and hamburgers float through their minds. This hunger seems to be the body's warning that it is about to empty its fuel tank.

After running another two miles dreaming of food, a sudden heavy lethargy overtakes the runner. His pace suddenly drops by one, two or three minutes per mile. After another mile at the slowest pace, great pains are felt in the legs. Each time the foot strikes the ground, it feels as though he has been struck by a bat across the thighs. The runner now either shuffles and walks to the finish in spite of the pain, or he quits.

213. Do all runners "hit the wall" in the marathon race?

No. The runners who are well trained, and who properly pace themselves, run through the finish line with no difficulty. It is largely a matter of developing a sufficiently high base level. Runners who train less than 50-60 miles per week are the ones who most often suffer in the last six miles.

214. How should I prepare for marathon racing?

I do not recommend that anyone attempt the marathon race until he has achieved two criteria in training:

1. He should have averaged at least 60 miles of running per week for at least the past three months.

2. He should take at least one long training run of from 25-30 miles.

The higher the average weekly training mileage, the less likely the runner is to "hit the wall" in the race. The long training runs give the runner confidence in his ability to stay on his feet for what will appear to be a very long period of time. These runs also teach him how his body reacts to long distances and deepen his respect for the race.

Frequent short races (less than 10 miles) are also valuable in the months prior to a marathon. Longer races will dig too deeply into the novice's energy stores.

215. I know of runners who have completed the marathon on far less training. Why shouldn't I?

I estimate that about half the marathoners in any race are doing themselves foolish harm. They are undertrained, and the excitement of a competitive marathon race provides no safe setting for such an unnatural and extended effort.

Many of them are injured in the months following the race. If the injury does not occur in the race itself, they rarely connect the two. Injury is born of excessive fatigue. After a hard race, the body is weakened. Follow this by several weeks of hard training, and a serious mechanical failure is likely.

216. How many days' rest are required before a marathon race?

Since the marathon race will dig far deeper into the runner's energy reserves than will shorter races, a longer easy period before the race is needed. I like to have three consecutive days before the race in which I only go two or three miles. In addition, there should be no long training runs within two weeks of the race.

217. What is "carbohydrate-loading?"

This is a special dietary scheme of recent years designed to increase the marathoner's stores of energy. Presumably, this will prevent him from "hitting the wall."

There are two phases to carbohydrate-loading:

1. *The depletion phase.* About one week prior to the marathon race, the runner runs a long hard run to empty his energy stores. He empties them further by going on a low-carbohydrate diet for the next few days. He eats

proteins (meat, eggs, cheese and milk) and fats, but little bread, fruit and vegetables.

2. *The loading phase.* A few days before the race, he reverses the diet. He now eats more carbohydrate, and less protein and fat.

218. Do you recommend carbohydrate loading?

No. I would not think it wise to severely alter one's diet prior to a hard race. Further, there is no real need for this. With proper training, the runner will not "hit the wall." Carbohydrate-loading is a desperate last-chance measure practiced by runners who should stay home and train rather than enter a marathon race.

Unfortunately, carbohydrate-loading is frequently a last-chance measure practiced by runners who should stay home and train rather than endure the torture of a marathon race without proper preparation.

219. What do you eat before a marathon race?

Most runners like a meal rich in carbohydrates but low in protein the night before the race. The traditional meal for marathoners is spaghetti. I follow this practice for two reasons. First, the meal agrees with my system and passes through me quickly. It is important to be able to have a thorough bowel movement in the morning of the race. Second, the meal seems to "stick to my bones." I do sense that I have a bit more energy from it.

Most marathon races start at noon or earlier. This means that there is little time to digest breakfast. I usually drink tea with honey and fruit juice, but have no solid food in the morning. A small bit of pastry probably does no harm.

220. Describe the start of a marathon race.

Most marathons today have a large starting field of run-ners. This means that they are packed several rows deep as they await the starter's gun. Fortunately, in most races the road is wide enough that there is little difficulty in passing runners when the occasion arises.

The start of all races, including the marathon, is much

too fast for 95% of the runners. The marathon differs from shorter races in that far more patience is required of the runner. Surrounded by hundreds of runners, the atmosphere is electrically charged, and it takes the greatest self-control to relax and settle into the proper speed that can be maintained to the finish.

The marathon race is sufficiently long that even the best-trained runner can crack in the final miles from starting too fast. It is absolutely essential to move off the starting line at the correct pace.

221. What should I do if I start too fast?

In spite of my greatest efforts, I frequently start my marathon races too fast. I realize this at about 3-5 miles when I sense that I am slightly forcing the pace. I must be completely relaxed and not "reaching out" until the final eight miles of the race.

Once I start too fast, and am aware of this fact, you would think that I would simply slow up. This is far easier said than done. It is as though you are caught in a great wind and cannot free yourself.

I usually must do something quite dramatic to brake my speed. I will be running at, say, 5:30 speed, and I will suddenly slow to 8:00 speed for about 100 yards. Many runners pass me in this short interval. I then slowly accelerate to the correct pace. Without this "braking" action, I find it impossible to ease up.

222. What do you think of during the race?

Thoughts should contribute to relaxation. I frequently hum mentally some pleasant melody that is appropriate for my running speed. Music certainly helps one to relax. Until 18 miles have been run, I fight all urges to be competitive.

When a runner moves up to my shoulder and challenges, I will deliberately ease up momentarily to prevent myself from engaging in a contest too early. This is very important, as it saves energy for the difficult final miles. I concentrate on my running form and try to strike the ground gently.

223. Should I eat or drink during the race?

The faster one runs, the more difficult it is to take in nourishment during the race. I generally don't like to eat or drink when I'm running near six-minute mile speed. On warm days, I prefer to throw available water over my head rather than drink it.

The quantity of fluid that should be replaced during the race itself is an individual matter. I personally drink little in the marathon, but I drink a great deal in the 50-miler. (This subject is discussed more fully in Chapter 13.)

If the final miles seem a bit difficult, a few sips of sugared iced tea seem to give me a lift.

224. Describe how it feels to run the last six miles of the marathon.

I have previously described the intense discomfort associated with poor preparation and pacing and the resultant "hitting-the-wall" syndrome. I will now describe the vista from the eyes of a runner who has his affairs well under control.

At the 20-mile mark, more than half the field has been reduced to a very slow run or walk. Runners are seen lined up before you, extending as far as the eye can see, and nearly all of them are "sitting ducks." You pass runner after runner, and none responds to your challenge. Your own weariness is forgotten when you see your opposition limping along the road. A full head of steam is built, and you rush to the finish line with the good feeling of a job properly executed.

After crossing the finish line, you grab your sweat suit and slowly run and walk briskly for 15-30 minutes before showering.

225. How frequently should I race the marathon?

I would not recommend racing this distance "all-out" more than twice each year. You can enter races more frequently with relatively little risk provided you run them as "easy races." (The method of running easy races is described in Chapter 10.)

226. I've heard of runners doing back-to-back marathons. Is this wise?

No man can recover from a hard marathon race in 24 hours. Rather, at least 24 days are needed by the best trained runners in the world.

Good runners can run back-to-back marathons provided they run them as easy training runs and not as competitive races. The most outstanding exponent of this procedure is the great Park Barner from Enola, Pa. Park is a rare runner who combines world-class ability with an extraordinary non-competitive attitude. Park doesn't care where he finishes in races; he simply likes to run.

His most outstanding double came in November 1974. On a Saturday in New York City, he finished second in the National AAU 50-Mile Championship in the time of 5:50:09. The next day, he was sixth in the Harrisburg Marathon, running 2:44:30.

227. Will racing the marathon make me slower at shorter distances?

The best marathon runners are good at all distance races. America's greatest-ever marathoner, Frank Shorter, frequently wins the National Cross-Country Championships and the AAU 10,000-meter track race.

Nevertheless, young runners should consider that the marathon requires considerable time for recovery. A marathon race in April could ruin his chances in the track championships in May. It would not be wise for a novice runner to enter a marathon race within three months of the major championships that concern him.

13

RACING ULTRA-MARATHONS

228. What is an ultra-marathon?

Any race longer than the marathon distance of 26 miles, 385 yards is called an ultra-marathon. The shortest commonly-run race of this type is at 50 kilometers (31.1 miles). However, I like to think of 50 kilometers as merely a long marathon.

The shortest ultra-marathon worthy of the name is the 50-miler. This is the most common race of this type in America today. There are also a few 100-kilometer races (62.2 miles). Now and then, a race of 100 miles or 24 hours appears.

229. Briefly, describe the history of ultra-marathoning.

Throughout recorded history there is mention of men who could cover great distances on foot in very short time. Usually, these men were associated with one of two professions, messengers and the military. We have already noted Pheidippides' run from Athens to Sparta, 125 miles in one day, in 490 B.C. He was a trained runner whose efforts were employed to carry important messages. Military men developed their long-distance power on long marches.

An aura of legend often surrounds their exploits. Jonas Cattel (1758—1854) became known as the "Paul Revere of South Jersey." He ran 10 miles through the night to warn the troops at Fort Mercer of an impending assault by the Hessians in 1777. At the age of 55, Cattel won a wager by running from Woodbury, N.J., to Cape May, a distance of 80 miles, in one day.

After the late 18th century, we find evidence of growing interest in a sport called "pedestrianism." In most cases, sums of money were wagered on the success of the pedestrian's claim that he could cover a particular long distance in a given time. At times, considerable money was at stake, and many of these efforts were recorded and survive to this day.

Among them, we find that Foster Powell covered 100 miles in 22 hours in 1788 in England. In 1806, the British Captain Barclay covered 100 miles in 19 hours. In 1808, he won a fortune by becoming the first man to walk one mile in each and every one of 1000 consecutive hours. This means that he had to walk one mile during each hour of the day, for 42 consecutive days!

A new era in the history of pedestrianism was initiated in 1874 when the Yankee, Edward Payson Weston, became the first man to walk 500 miles in six days. This he achieved on a small indoor track in Newark, N.J. The sporting world went mad over this performance, and Weston became the toast of both America and Britain.

The British sporting gentleman Sir John D. Astley established a prize belt for the "Pedestrian Championship of the World." During the years 1877—79, there were five struggles for the belt. In each case, the contest was staged indoors on a track measuring about eight laps to the mile. Starting at midnight on Monday morning and continuing for 144 consecutive hours until midnight Saturday, the contestants would walk, run, eat and sleep in an effort to cover the greatest mileage. Enormous crowds came to watch and wager on the contests. The victorious pedestrian became a national hero and a wealthy man.

The greatest distance ever achieved in one of these

six-day contests was 623¾ miles by George Littlewood at Madison Square Garden, New York City in 1888.

In the 1920s, Arthur Newton, a professional runner from Rhodesia, broke all existing records from 50 miles to 24 hours. These include: 50 miles, 5:38:42; 100 miles, 14:06:00; and 24 hours, 152 miles, 540 yards.

The 52-mile London-to-Brighton race was revived by the British RRC in the early 1950s and has been held every year since. It has been a source of encouragement to ultra-marathoners during the past three decades.

The modern era of ultra-marathoning in the United States began in 1962 when Ted Corbitt of New York City finished fourth in the London-to-Brighton run. Slowly, ultra-marathon races began to emerge here and there in America. In addition to several remarkable runs on the London-to-Brighton course, Corbitt ran the following which are still American records: 100 miles, 13:33:06 in 1969; 24 hours, 134.7 miles in 1973. The book *Corbitt* by John Chodes chronicles his running experiences and has been an inspiration to runners everywhere.

230. Who was the greatest ultra-marathoner of all time?

My good friend Edward Dodd and I have spent several years researching the exploits of the oldtime pedestrians. While it is never possible to answer such a question with absolute certainty, it appears to us that this honor should go to the great British champion Charles Rowell.

Rowell was born in 1854. He stood 5'6" and weighed 140 pounds. He was twice winner of the Astley Belt for the "Long-Distance Championship of the World" which he secured in six-day contests at Madison Square Garden. These victories gave him over $50,000 in prize money. Rowell retired the Belt in 1879, a wealthy man.

In 1882, he returned to New York City for what he saw as his final and greatest performance. A six-day contest would take place in Madison Square Garden on the week of Feb. 27-March 4, and Rowell was secretly running 40 miles per day in the hope of establishing an incredible record of 700 miles in six days.

Rowell set to work, covering the first 100 miles in 13:26:30. (This is some seven minutes better than the present American record!) He retired the first day after being on the track for 22.5 hours and covering 150 miles, 395 yards. (The present world record for 24 hours was set in 1973 by Ron Bentley of Great Britain. It is only 11 miles further than Rowell's mark! Remember, Rowell did not run the last 1½ hours of the day. Surely he could have matched steps with Bentley.)

Rowell ran on to record: 200 miles in 35:09:28; 300 miles in 58:17:06; 258 miles, 220 yards in 48 hours; and 353 miles, 220 yards in 72 hours.

After the third day, Rowell accidentally drank a cup of warm vinegar. His stomach revolted and he was forced to retire from the contest. Nevertheless, we believe that his performance here is unmatched in the history of ultramarathoning. There is no one alive today who could match Rowell's steps.

231. Have you found the performances of a particular pedestrian to be very enlightening?

Yes, the exploits of Edward Payson Weston have been both revealing and inspirational. Weston was born in Providence, R.I. in 1839. He was a walker, not a runner. In fact, he did not utilize the "heel and toe" style used today by race walkers. Rather he walked as you and I do, only very rapidly.

Weston's career as a professional pedestrian spanned 1861—1913, a full 52 years in one of the most difficult sports ever seen. How did he survive? Weston knew how to distribute his energy. He knew when to go hard and when to take it easy. More often than not, he failed to win the many contests he started. However, when Weston was right, he was magnificent.

A good example occurred in the fourth Astley Belt for the Pedestrian Championship of the World at six days in London in 1879. Weston was 40 years old. He had watched Charles Rowell and realized that a good walker could never beat a good runner. Weston tried running and found that he could master it quite well.

MR. WESTON IN HIS TWENTY-NINTH YEAR AS HE APPEARED IN HIS PORTLAND-CHICAGO WALK IN 1867.

Weston as he walked from Portland, Maine, to Chicago in 1867 at age 29. (Photo courtesy of Ed Dodd)

Poster advertising Weston's 6-day exhibition walk in London. (Photo courtesy of Ed Dodd)

Weston in his final years. He died at the age of 90 when he was struck by a taxi. (Photo courtesy of Ed Dodd)

Charles Rowell of England leads during the third contest for the Astley Belt—Pedestrian Championship of the World—at Madison Square Garden, March, 1879. The contest lasted six consecutive days. (Photo courtesy of Ed Dodd)

Weston's rainy day garb as he walked across the USA at age 70. (Photo courtesy of Ed Dodd)

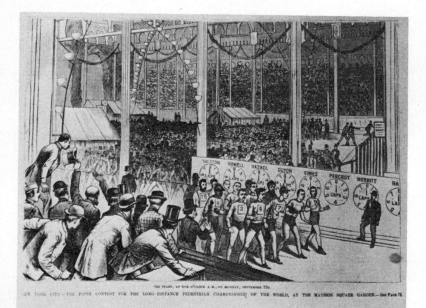

Start of the fifth Astley Belt struggle for the Pedestrian 6-day Championship of the World at Madison Square Garden, September 22, 1879. (Photo courtesy of Ed Dodd)

Weston paced himself so well that on the final day of the contest he looked fresher than ever. He did his 501st mile in 7:39 and his 526th in 7:37. He went on to set a new world record of 550 miles. Never before or since did a pedestrian look so magnificent on the last day of a six-day contest.

In 1909, at the age of 70, he walked a route covering 3900 miles from New York to San Francisco in 105 days. The next year, he walked back from Los Angeles to New York, 3600 miles in 77 days. The entire country was captivated by the old man's spirit. The *New York Times* carried a daily report of his progress. Many adults who watched him pass remarked that they had seen him go by years before when they were but children. Frequently, he lectured in the churches, talking on "The Vicissitudes of a Walker." Reporters of the day described this speech as very humorous and in the style of Mark Twain.

In the year 1927, Weston was struck by a New York City taxi. He died on May 13, 1929, at the age of 90.

232. Do many runners participate in the ultra-marathons?

No. In spite of the tremendous growth that has been seen at the marathon and shorter distances in recent years, the ultra-marathons fail to attract entrants.

For example, in October 1976, 1485 runners finished the New York City Marathon. Two weeks later, in the same city, the most important ultra-marathon of the year took place, the National AAU 50-Mile Championship. Only 17 runners finished the race. For every 100 men who finish the marathon, only one will successfully finish 50 miles.

233. What has been your ultra-marathon experience?

My first race was the National RRC 50-Mile Championship on Thanksgiving Day, 1967, in Poughkeepsie, N.Y. There was a freezing rain throughout the race. As I mentioned before, a cold rain is an asset to the novice. It prevents

dehydration, and thus less experience is needed to successfully conserve one's strength to finish those last faraway
miles. I won the race in 5:52:33.

This victory left me badly beaten. My legs were stiff for a
week. I felt sick and weak. I became "gun-shy" and did
not enter another 50-miler until November 1974, when I
ran 6:12:55 at New York City. I ran very conservatively
here and finished in eighth place.

I was surprised to find that I was not even stiff the next
day and was able to resume normal training immediately. I
then realized that I could make an easy race out of even
this long distance. Since then, I have learned how to do
this with my distance.

My remaining 50-mile races include the following:

Date	Location	Place	Time
8/9/75	Ft. Meade, Md. (track)	1st	5:49:14
9/26/76	Baltimore	3rd	6:57:30
11/6/76	New York City	12th	6:38:11
8/6/77	Ft. Meade, Md.	2nd	5:51:13
9/18/77	Copper Harbor, Mich.	5th	6:29:25

On Dec. 9-10, 1976, I tried a solo 24-hour track performance. I managed 100 miles in 18:19:27 and a total of
114 miles for the full day. This proved to be one of the
most interesting events I've ever tried.

234. Are ultra-marathoners crazy?

I am frequently told I am crazy, even by marathon runners!
Have you noticed that the sprinter thinks the miler is crazy,
the miler thinks the six-miler is mad, and the six-miler
thinks the marathoner is nuts. Need I go on?

235. How do you train for the ultra-marathons?

Training for these races does not differ significantly from
training for the marathon and shorter races. What is
needed is many years of solid base training built on long,
slow runs. Here, there is no substitute for work in quantity.

There are no good ultra-marathoners who run only 25 miles per week. Many years of running experience also have their reward in these races.

While I only run about 50 miles per week during the winter, I am able to double this amount in the late spring and race 50 miles well by the end of the summer. I would not be able to "crash-train" in this way were it not for the fact that I've been no stranger to the road and track for the past 23 years.

However, the prospective ultra-marathoner should try these very long distances in training before he attempts them in races. While this is not necessary from a physical standpoint, it is from a psychological one. If the longest distance you have ever run is 26 miles, and you find yourself standing at the start of a 50-miler, you will find it a very intimidating experience. It is impossible to conceive of running the full marathon distance twice!

236. Describe in detail an ultra-marathon training run.

The purpose of this run is to convince the runner that he can stay on his feet for hours and hours. He will endeavor to cover a very long distance *and still be relatively fresh* after the run. He should be able to resume normal training in a day or two after this.

How can you cover 50 miles without exhausting yourself? You must mix a generous dose of walking with the running. Also, you must drink fluids liberally to ward off dehydration.

The entire experience should be looked upon as a day of fun. Never will the runner allow himself to get tired.

I like to lay out a course that will take me past many stores and gas stations where I can purchase drinks, usually soda. I carry about $30 with me in change and bills. I want to be able to get a cab home if necessary. I usually stop every 20 minutes, buy a drink and walk for five minutes while working it down. Then I run for 20 minutes, drink and walk for five, etc. I enjoy this very much and have taught myself that I can always finish one of these incredibly long races.

237. Can I walk during the actual race?

Yes, and it is a good idea to plan on this if you feel it is necessary. It would be difficult to run 50 miles faster than 6:30 and in addition do a considerable quantity of walking. However, 50 miles in 7-8 hours is very respectable time, and can be achieved with large amounts of walking mixed with running.

I have never used walking in my 50-mile races, but this is due to the many years of training I have for support. I recommend that runners with less experience learn to walk and run in their early attempts at these races. In this way, they will finish with plenty of energy to spare.

238. How does one prepare in the days before the race? What about food and rest?

The number of days needed for rest, and the pre-race meals are essentially the same as those used before marathon races. (These were considered in Chapter 12.)

239. How do you prepare psychologically for these races?

This is a very important concern. Without the proper outlook, I become tense and unable to relax properly. If I am the least bit tense at the start of these races, I will lose large amounts of energy that will be so badly needed in the final miles.

First, I view the race as a "fun" experience. I promise myself that by going out at a careful, easy pace, I will not suffer in the final miles but will run to the finish line looking strong and fresh.

I find it necessary to concentrate on the conclusion of the race. If I do not keep the finish in mind, I usually go out too fast and quit later. I personally cannot conceive of running 50 miles. Although I have done it many times in training and racing, the distance still awes me.

I can, however, mentally, grasp the time necessary to complete the race. This serves exactly the same purpose. For example, if I am racing 50 miles and the race starts at 6 a.m., then I know that I will finish at about noon. This six-hour time interval can be appreciated, since I experience it every day.

As the race progresses, I look at the time and always relate it to the finish at noon. In this way, I relax and ignore the fact that this or that runner is so many miles ahead of me. I know that my first job is to get to the finish line, and I won't make it in good shape if I foolishly miscalculate the pace.

240. Can the ultra-marathoner have his own private handler during the race?

Fortunately, yes. International rules forbid the use of handlers in races up to the marathon distance. They even require that aid stations be about five kilometers apart and that competitors risk disqualification if they accept any help between stations. These rules are archaic and should be ignored.

The ultra-marathons have been free of such absurd rules, because they are not Olympic events. The runners themselves have set up rules which are appropriate for this sport.

241. What are the handler's duties?

The handler should know his runner very well. At least one day before the race, the handler and runner should sit down and discuss every detail of the race plan. Here is a list of the items I usually discuss with my handler:

1. If it is a road race, I usually prefer that he have a car rather than a bicycle. I ask him not to follow me as I run down the road, as this could create a traffic hazard. I ask that he stop off the road every two or three miles and supply me with drinks or sponges. If the weather is very hot, it might be necessary for him to stop much more frequently.

2. Supply the handler with all necessary drinks, sponges, water containers, etc. Make provision for refills.

3. Supply the handler with necessary changes of shoes and clothes. Also, supply first-aid items like petroleum jelly and tape.

4. Give the handler a good idea of your racing plans and alternatives. You might want him to give you periodic reports of the positions of your competitors.

5. While the handler might be "your man," I feel that it is unsportsmanlike to refuse assistance to any competitor who requests it. To be sure, it is not your handler's job to ask every runner if he wants help, but he should provide help to another competitor if it is specifically requested and does not interfere in a material way with his duty to assist you.

242. Describe in detail how you feel while you race 50 miles.

Before the race, I try to adjust my mind for the task at hand. I think gentle, easy thoughts. I absolutely refuse to allow myself to "race" my competitors. The race will dictate its own outcome. I must become highly tuned to myself and my environment. I must be able to detect the slightest tensions so that they can be released in time. I imagine that all nature is animate. I ask the road to soften my steps. I ask the trees to give me shade. I ask the breeze to make me cool.

Finally, the gun is fired and we are off. I like to see the field run away from me. Then, I'm sure that my pace is not too fast. At times, I find myself leading. This makes me worry that I am going too hard. No matter how well trained you are, in races of this length anyone can be forced to quit by not respecting the distance.

Now that the race is underway, I must settle down to a long, gentle coasting through the first 35 miles. Marathoners say that their race begins at 20 miles. For 50 milers, the race begins at 35. This will take some four hours! One must be incredibly patient.

Runners I hope to beat are out of sight, but I must not worry. If I'm worthy to beat them, they will come back in due course. I watch the long hours pass, running gently to the rhythm of whatever tune my mind has captured that day. (I remember one National 50-Mile Championship in which I heard with my mind's ear "Whistle While You Work" from Walt Disney's "Snow White"!)

By 35 miles, the race begins to take form. Most of the hot early starters have now retired. The serious runners remain on the road. By 40 miles, the race is always getting tough. Ten more miles; it seems like forever. Slowly, the miles are run, one by one. There are so few starters in these races that one often doesn't see another runner for miles and miles.

Finally, I cross the finish line. There is an immense feeling of satisfaction with a really hard job completed. I must now walk briskly for about a half-hour, in spite of my weariness. This will greatly reduce tomorrow's stiffness.

243. Why did you attempt a 24-hour run?

For several years, I had been studying the performances of the great pedestrians of the 19th century. Here, I saw men competing in frequent six-day races. On one occasion, Edward Payson Weston finished one six-day race on a Saturday evening, only to follow it by starting another six-day race on Monday with but one day's rest!

How was it possible for men to compete in so many long races? As I studied further, I began to realize that by the appropriate introduction of walking, these distances could be covered with only a tiny fraction of the fatigue that is generated by continuous running. I experimented with running mixed with walking, and the theory seemed to be true.

I wanted very much to put these ideas to an acid test, and the 24-hour run would provide that opportunity.

244. I read the description of the 24-hour run in John Chodes book *Corbitt*. It seemed like hell! Must it be that way?

It was hell for most of these men, because they ran the entire distance, start to finish. This is a mistake for all but the most incredibly well-prepared runners. It may even be a mistake for them.

By learning how to walk and run, one can add needed rest periods during the day without losing too much ground. This completely changes the complexion of the event and makes it much more humane.

245. How did you prepare psychologically for the 24-hour run?

Mental preparation for these long runs is very important. I do not like being weary; I do not like suffering; I do not like pain. The 24-hour run would have none of this. It was to be one of the most "fun" days of my life. I would take an entire 24 hours and do nothing but my favorite activities— running and walking.

I promised myself that it would be a "go as you please" affair. This phrase was used in the past century to describe contests where the entrants ran, walked, ate and slept at will, right on the athletic field. Besides, if I got tired, how was I going to finish 24 hours? Impossible! Thus, I would stay fresh and feel good for the entire day.

I had nothing to fear. I was like a boy before Christmas!

246. What other preparations were necessary for the 24-hour run?

One of the really interesting aspects of the 24-hour run is the challenge it provides in trying to maximize the distance you can cover. You have all these variables to plan for:

1. When and how fast should I run?
2. When and how fast should I walk?
3. Should I take complete rests?
4. When should I eat and drink? What foods should I use?

I decided to remain flexible. I drew up three plans based on my training experience:

Plan One: I would run seven laps then walk one, run seven, walk one, etc. The run would simply be as relaxed and easy as my legs themselves dictated.

Plan Two: I would run three laps, then walk one.

Plan Three: I would run one lap, then walk one, run one, then walk one, etc.

I decided to drink tea and orange juice mixed with sugar, as I do in my 50 milers. I also decided to eat dates. After finishing 100 miles, I decided to treat myself to a spaghetti meal and a brief rest.

247. Describe your experiences during the 24-hour run.

I did not sleep at all the night before. I just couldn't wait to get on that track.

We started at 5 a.m. on a cold, clear December morning. Fortunately, there was no wind. It was about 20 degrees, and thus I wore a hat, gloves and ski pajamas to cover my legs.

The freshman class at Glassboro State College, where I teach, holds an annual "Project Santa" fund raising drive for needy families in the area. Various professors do special stunts for the project to help raise money. This was to be my contribution. It attracted a great deal of attention throughout the campus and the local press, radio and television. I had several friends start with me and run portions of the distance throughout the day.

I was too excited to start walking as planned after the first seven laps, so I decided to wait until my nerves quieted. By the seventh mile, I finally relaxed and walked my first lap. From this point on, I followed Plan One until 100 miles were covered. I walked a quarter-mile during every two miles.

Gradually, the light of dawn spread over the cinder track. I had thought before the run of the great beauty of watching the sun rise and set, and the night close in darkly while the run went ever on. I did my best to relax and stay fresh. About every half-hour, I reversed direction on the track. This helped in a small way to change the vista. But more importantly, it produces a change in the angle at which the legs were twisted when I rounded the turn. (The great pedestrians of the past century had done this.)

When we started, the track was firm and fairly flat. As the sun warmed it, however, ice crystals that were in the cinders began to melt, and the track slowly began to flood. By noon, the water was so deep on the inside lane that it became necessary to use the very outside of the track.

This was no real problem, for the extra distance run could easily be computed. The real problem was the track itself. It was now very soft and full of footprints. When the sun dropped low in the late afternoon, the water froze solid again, and the mushy footprints became hard ruts. It felt like running on rough concrete. Fortunately, a very small section on the very outside of the track remained tolerable throughout the full 24 hours. I was very worried however, throughout the day.

I passed 50 miles in 8:08:13 feeling rather good. I then left the track for a bowel movement in the fieldhouse which is only about 50 yards away.

The sun began to set at about 70 miles. It was a dramatically beautiful sight, and I was fresh enough to really enjoy it. But the freezing ruts on the track broke my concentration. Students are night people, and now many more arrived to run a few laps, wish me well or just watch.

At 80 miles, I began to grow weary. For the first time, I was no longer comfortable. Now I was only averaging five miles per hour, and it would be four long hours before I made 100 miles. I really wanted to stop and take a rest, but I thought it unwise.

After 95 miles the anticipation of covering 100 miles overcame all weariness. I envisioned the ghosts of Weston, Rowell and the other great pedestrians of the past century watching me. What did they think? Was I now worthy of the title "pedestrian"?

Finally the 100-mile mark was reached. Our college president was on hand with many students and reporters to offer congratulations. I was weary but very, very pleased. I went inside the field house, changed all my clothes and sat down to a warm spaghetti dinner. I then took a 10-minute nap and left again for the track.

I had been off the track for 57 minutes, and when I returned I found to my horror that I could no longer run. Walking was comfortable, but when I tried running my legs felt as though they were incredibly heavy. There was no pain and no stiffness, just great weight in my legs. Thus, I walked another 14 miles until the 24 hours were complete. Fortunately, it was a cold, clear, still night. The cold air kept me awake.

248. How did you feel in the days following the 24-hour run?

Surprisingly good. I never became stiff! There was no leg soreness. I was a bit weary and my eyes were quite red when I arrived home at 6 a.m. However, after a few naps during the day my eyes grew clear and I felt much better. I took two days off from training and resumed normal work on the third day.

249. What did you learn from your experience in the 24-hour run?

This event taught me an important lesson. By the introduction of walking, great distances can be covered with relatively little fatigue. The walking very much aids the recovery process.

I am now convinced that the human body was not designed for long, continuous running, even at a slow pace. Man can cover great distances in reasonably fast time without undue fatigue—if he walks the entire way, or mixes running and walking. The pedestrians of the past centuries knew this. But we are the products of the automobile age in which this lesson has been lost.

14
PREDICTING YOUR TIMES

250. What is the purpose of this chapter?

In this chapter, I demonstrate how the chart shown in Figure One can be used to determine a number of interesting predictions concerning running performance. You will be able to determine the answers to questions like the following:

1. Which is the better performance, three miles in 15 minutes or six miles in 31 minutes?

2. Today, you ran the mile in 4:40. What time would you have run for three miles?

3. What will the world record for six miles be in the year 1990?

In addition, this chart assigns a "score" to each running performance. For example, it attaches the score "1970" to a six-mile run in the time of 27:00. For world-class performances, the score itself is approximately the year in which the world record equalled this performance.

251. What is the meaning of the lines on Figure One?

There are three sets of lines on Figure One. These are the vertical set, the horizontal set and the diagonal set.

FIGURE 1

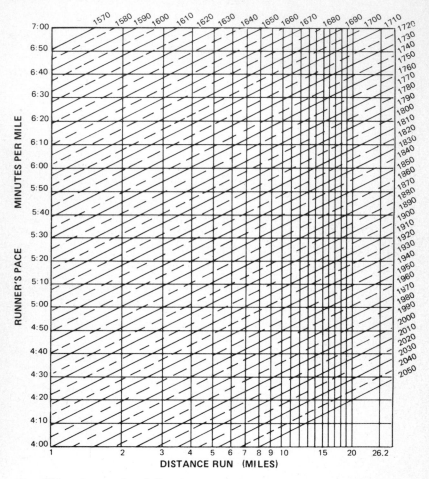

They have the following meanings:

1. *Vertical lines:* These identify the distance the runner has raced in miles. These distances are read along the bottom of the graph. Notice that the separation between the numbers on the bottom scale grows less and less as you move from left to right. The separation between one and two miles is much wider than the separation between nine and 10 miles. Technically, this is called a "logarithmic" scale.

2. *Horizontal lines:* These identify the runner's pace in minutes and seconds per mile. The scale along the left

edge of the graph identifies the pace associated with each of these lines.

3. *Diagonal lines:* These identify the runner's performance score. The scale along the right and top edges of the graph identifies the score associated with each of these lines.

252. How do you read the chart in Figure One?

This is best understood by examples.

Example One: Look at the point marked "A" in Figure Two. The vertical line through this point reads "2 miles" on the scale at the bottom of the graph. The horizontal line through this point reads "5 minutes per mile" on the scale at the left. The diagonal line through the Point A reads score "1850" on the right edge of the graph. This means that a runner who runs two miles at the pace of five minutes per mile merits the performance score of 1850. Thus, two miles run in 10 minutes gets the score 1850.

Example Two: The point marked "B" in Figure Two identifies a run of 10 miles (vertical line and bottom scale) at the pace of 4:50 per mile (horizontal line and left scale), which earns the performance score of 1950 (diagonal line and right edge scale). Thus, a runner who does 10 miles in the time of 48:20 merits the score 1950. It is interesting to note that the world record for 10 miles in 1951 was about 48:12. This illustrates the fact that for very fast performances, the score earned is approximately the year this was the world record.

Example Three: A runner does 20 miles in the time 2:01:00. What is his performance score? We must first determine his pace in minutes and seconds per mile, in this case 6:03. Next, we locate this performance on the graph. We find the vertical line associated with 20 miles and the horizontal line associated with 6:03 per mile. Because there is a horizontal line for 6:00 and for 6:10, but none for 6:03, we must imagine where this line would be between the above two. The intersection of the lines is the point marked "C" on Figure Two. The diagonal line through this point shows that it earns the performance score 1820. (In this case, the score does not indicate that the world record was 2:01 in the year 1820. Only scores over 1920 closely approximate world records.)

253. How can you decide which of two performances is better?

Using the graph in Figure One, this is easy. We simply determine the score for each of the two performances. The run with the higher score is superior.

Example One: Which is better, three miles in 15 minutes or six miles in 31 minutes? From Figure One, we see that a 15-minute three-miler (5:00 per mile) earns the score 1870. We also see that a 31-minute six-miler (5:10 per mile) earns the score 1880. Thus, the six-mile performance is superior. Of course, this assumes that both runs occurred under identical conditions. If the three-miler was run on a bad cinder track, while the six was on a fine all-weather surface, then the three might be superior.

Example Two: Which is faster, a marathon in three hours or 10 miles in one hour? A three-hour marathon is run at 6:52 pace. Using Figure One, we see that this marathon merits the score of about 1728. The one-hour 10-miler is at the pace 6:00. It merits the score of about 1796. Thus, the 10-mile run is superior.

Does this mean that a runner who can do 60 minutes for 10 miles will break three hours for the marathon? Not always; he must have the necessary training to carry his performance level up to the marathon distance. Runners who do very low weekly mileage will not be able to hold their standard performance over as wide a range of distances as those who do high mileages.

254. How can I predict my own performances?

Suppose you know your best time for a given distance. You can predict how fast you will run other distances (under equivalent conditions) by assuming that your performance score will remain the same for all events. This assumption has been found to be very accurate in practice.

FIGURE 2

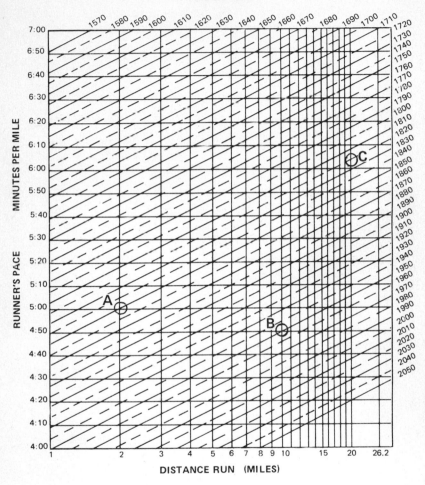

DISTANCE RUN (MILES)

Again, we assume that the runner is trained effectively for the entire range of distances that he considers. A person who runs 25 miles per week will not run a marathon with the same performance score that he runs three miles.

Example: Today, I raced six miles in 33:00. I believe this to be one of my finest races. How fast would I have run three miles today?

This performance was run at the pace of 5:30 per mile. It is identified as point "A" on Figure Three. This point is

7:30
7:20 -
7:10 -

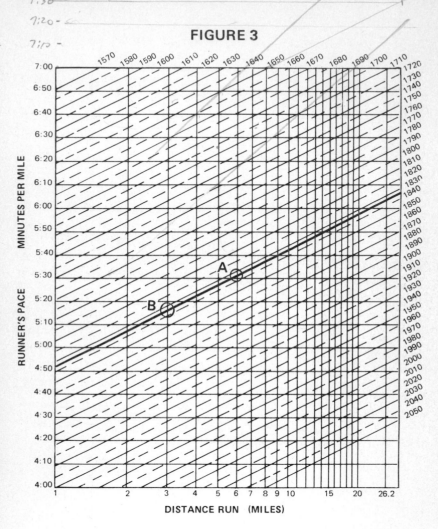

FIGURE 3

MINUTES PER MILE

RUNNER'S PACE

DISTANCE RUN (MILES)

just above the 1840 score line, so it merits a score of
approximately 1838. Draw a straight line through Point A
parallel to the diagonal lines as shown in Figure Three.
This is your *performance level line.* It predicts how you can
race from one mile to the marathon. Point B identifies the
spot where your performance level line of 1838 crosses the
vertical three mile line. At point B, the pace reads 5:15.
Thus, you would most likely have run three miles in 15:45
today.

255. How can you predict future world records in distance running?

Since performance scores of 1920 and greater also tell the year in which the world record was at this very score, it seems reasonable to assume that scores for future years will do the same. Indeed, I first made this observation in 1964, and for the past 13 years it has proven to be quite accurate.

Naturally, there must be some limit beyond which man cannot go. That limit, however, appears to be far, far in the future. Track performances have improved at the rate of one-half second per mile per year since 1920. The rate has not declined for 50 years. We can expect, therefore, that the present records are still far from the ultimate in human potential.

Example One: Will we ever see a sub-8:00 two-mile performance? Figure One shows that two miles run at the rate of four minutes to the mile earns the score of about 1982. This means that such a performance will probably be seen in the early or middle 1980s. It will be overdue by 1990.

Example Two: Will we ever see a sub-two-hour marathon? To run the marathon in two hours requires a 4:34 pace. This earns a performance level of 2033. I will be 93 years old then! I hope to see it done, but I'm not counting on it. It will be far harder to run the sub-two-marathon than it will to run the sub-eight two-mile.

FINAL THOUGHTS

My journey is not finished. Thus far, if my miles were stretched end to end around the earth's circumference, they would circle the globe twice. I have learned important lessons from these many steps, most of which I have tried to clarify in the preceding pages.

There is, however, a single, simple message that might have been lost in the jungle of specific questions on training, diet, dress, etc. *We should learn to listen to our bodies; we should have greater respect for our intuitive feelings.*

All too quickly, we turn for technical answers to questions that often have a more satisfying intuitive solution. Ancient man personified the forces of nature. He made gods of the sun, the sea and the wind. These give life a color and adventure in which he was able to interpret solutions for his everyday needs.

When fighting a desperate struggle to hold my speed in the final miles of a 50-mile race, I have seen myself ask the trees for shade and the road to soften its surface. Personifying the forces of nature makes the world seem all the more colorful and full of fantasy. This is just the thing needed when your entire body is locked in a mad physical fight.

It is time to put an end to words. I am but 37 years old, and my journey is not yet complete. The joy of the road calls me. There is no rhythm to compare with a gentle flowing stride; there is no symphony as sweet as our own inner harmonies.

Index

This index refers to question numbers and not page numbers.

weight
  difficulty losing—**148**
  effect on racing—**140**
  fluids and reductions—**144**
  gain after racing—**189**
  loss—**141**
  reducing, length of time of—**146**
  and running—**139**
  and sharpening—**52**
  specific reducing
    diets—**142, 143**
  and training—**92**
  training while dieting—**145**
well-being
  feeling after workouts—**63**
  and injury prevention—**97, 100**
Weston, Edward Payson
  biography—**231**
  inspiration—**243**
  and pedestrianism—**229**
when to run—**76, 78**
where to run—**70**
White, Max—**149**
Windsor Castle—**210**
winter
  reduced mileage in—**47**
  see also "cold weather"
women, in racing—**170**
Woodbury, N.J.—**229**
workouts—see "training"
world records, prediction
  of—**250-255**

—Y—

young, runners and racing—**169**

—Z—

Zatopek, Emil—**83**

ABOUT THE AUTHOR

Tom Osler was born on April 26, 1940, in Camden, N.J. He began his running career as a miler in high school at the age of 14 and has continued without interruption for the past 24 years. He is a veteran of more than 750 races ranging in distance from one mile to 114 miles. He was winner of three national championships: the AAU 25 Kilometers in 1965, the AAU 30 Kilometers in 1967 and the RRC 50 Miles in 1967. Were his 50,000 training miles placed end to end about the earth's equator, they would circle the globe twice. He has organized numerous races at all distances, been Road Runner's Club president in both Philadelphia and Albany, N.Y., and now serves on the AAU Standards Committee which certifies the accuracy of road racing courses. He is author of the booklet *The Conditioning of Distance Runners* as well as numerous articles on this sport.

Osler has a Ph.D. in mathematics from New York University and is an associate professor at Glassboro State College where he teaches mathematics and does research. He is married and has two sons.